Lasted Another Year Despite A Pandemic

STEVE N ALLEN

Copyright © 2020 Steve N Allen

All rights reserved.

DEDICATION

To a special person who helped with all this.

CONTENTS

	Introduction	i
1	January	1
2	February	17
3	March	34
4	April	47
5	May	61
6	June	75
7	July	85
8	August	95
9	September	103
10	October	118
11	November	129
12	December	141

INTRODUCTION

For the last few years I have been writing newspaper columns for several papers. Without realising it they form a record of what we went through.

Each year I have compiled the columns to make a book of that year. I jokingly gave the previous books titles based on the fact we survived that year. This time, it's less of a joke. Making it to the end was an actual accomplishment.

Not everyone did. The number of people who died of coronavirus is shocking. I lost a dear family member in 2020 too. It has been a difficult time.

This review of our last twelve months has a strong and obvious theme but in the dark there were glimmers of light, hope, silliness and mockery. This is my view of the last year.

1 JANUARY

It's An Honour

The New Year makes us think of getting rid of the old and welcoming in the new, which is why it's strange that it brings with it another New Year Honours list. It is an outdated concept we get from the Normans. If we don't end it soon we run the risk of having leftovers from a feudal system and hover-jet cars at the same time.

Some of these awards go to worthy people. There will be philanthropists and charity workers who get an honour but I am fairly sure some letters after their name is not why they started this; for them doing good is the goal.

As with any mention of change there will be people who push back, so let me address some of your issues. You may hope to receive one yourself in the future. It could give you something to finally impress the snobbier members of your family. You could get the same effect by purchasing a big car.

You may be happy that we still kept the system till 2020 because without it Nigel Farage wouldn't have felt like he missed out on something quite as much. You're just being mean.

You may be happy that the addresses of the rich and famous were leaked online by mistake. Don't worry, Government departments are always leaving laptops on trains, there will still be data leaks.

Besides, it can't be that hard to spot Sir Elton John's house, I would guess it stands out a fair bit from the rest in the street.

It's not just the celebs who had personal data released. Sports stars like the Olympic Taekwondo champion Jade Jones was on that list this year. Although having seen her compete you'd feel sorry for any burglars who chanced their soon-to-be-broken arm.

Even if you like the honours list ask yourself if we really need it. A knighthood makes sense when you're sending people into battle on horseback but if your realm needs defending by Sir Elton John you may have bigger problems.

For the entertainers the reward is their privileged life. For the sports stars they already get medals and trophies. For the people who work for a good cause the reward should be the results of their work.

If we did away with the whole system we would still have all of these people but we wouldn't have a system that, rightly or wrongly, can be seen as a way of a Government rewarding people for their favours.

Yes, you guessed it, I didn't get anything in this year's honours list. That means you'll have to find another way to get my home address.

Clap Your Hands

Are you happy? There are many ways to answer that question but if you thought, "It's none of your business, Steve," you were spot on.

That's why I have been concerned by the news that a piece of technology has been invented that will let bosses know if their employees are in a good mood. The system can read micro-expressions on people's faces that give away how they feel.

I don't have a problem with the technology. It would be useful to have an app that could tell you how someone is really feeling so when you ask your other half if they're OK and they say, "Fine," you could whip out the app, get the reading and see if it's best to leave the house for a few hours.

It's the use of this technology at work that worries me. You don't want your mood being brought up in your annual review. This is one step beyond the thought police, this is the feeling police.

There are some questions you don't want the answer to. Are your employees happy? Probably not. They're at work and their boss is monitoring their face.

The firm behind this says the tech will let them help staff with any issues, but we all know where this will end. Studies link happiness with productivity so unless you're happy every day at work the boss will dock your pay.

We will end up in a world where everyone has a fixed grin. In shops people will be over-polite. It'll be like living in America. I worry for the future of miserable-faced people like myself.

Then I read further and found that the company trying this, RotaCloud, is based in Yorkshire. If they won't employ dour people up there they'll have to shut. We're safe. And I almost look happy about it.

The Rules

I am a rule follower. I follow the direction of the arrows in a car park. I'm that kind of guy.

Therefore, if I think a rule is silly it's likely that the rule is at fault. That's why I think the Amazon driver who was in the news for refusing to deliver a bottle of sherry to a 92-year-old woman because she couldn't provide ID was very much in the wrong.

Louise Wilkinson's grandson had sent her the £8.50 bottle of Harvey's Bristol Cream along with a jigsaw puzzle but the driver requested photo identification before he could hand over the alcohol.

Why stop there? The jigsaw would say on the box that it was for anyone aged 3+ because of the small parts. ID her for that while you're at it.

I understand there would be a rule in place from the company saying you should ask for ID before handing over alcohol but there should be a rule for common sense. I haven't seen a picture of the lady in question but even if she was a really young-looking 92-year-old, a right stunner, you'd still know she was over 18.

What he was worried about? Maybe he had recently watched The Curious Case of Benjamin Button and was worried he was about to give booze to someone who'd just been born.

If the rule is that they should ask everyone, regardless of any obvious evidence, they are making the world a worse place. We have all known someone who turns up to work looking pleased with themselves. You try to avoid asking but eventually you give in and they tell you they were asked for ID when they tried to buy wine.

It's the most annoying humble-brag. It's often someone in

their thirties boasting to the whole office that someone thought they looked as young as a teenager.

At least the Challenge 25 rule that shops use, meaning they will ask for ID if you look 25, waters down the implied compliment of being age-checked.

To make things worse, when the driver returned with the slightly more aged bottle of sherry the next day Ms Wilkinson had found her bus pass but he still wouldn't hand over her tipple because that form of ID wasn't on the official list of acceptable identification.

Surely that's the best one. She looks old enough, she has a form of ID that only pensioners would have, and she clearly wasn't driving that day so hand over the booze.

Even as a rule-follower I have to say it's people like that who are making us need a drink.

The Tech Crunch

Technology has changed our lives. We live longer, we travel faster, we only see the tops of teenagers' heads because they're looking down at their phone. If you want to know how technology will change us even further, then wait no longer, the Consumer Electronics Show is taking place in Las Vegas.

Not everything predicted there will come true. Tech is hard to get right. I remember watching Tomorrow's World when I was growing up and they had robots that could play snooker. Here we are in 2020 still playing snooker manually like cavemen.

Some of the advancements at this year's show are amazing. Proctor & Gamble have created artificial intelligence that can tell if you have a spot. For years we were worried that AI would rise up against us and enslave mankind but now we realise it'll just be judgemental about our looks. I would have said that being nasty about someone's appearance is something we humans are already really good at but it's nice to know we'll have help.

Lenovo has released what it's called the world's first foldable laptop, which has made me really worried about what I have been doing to mine when I close it.

LG has released a "rollable" TV that has a flexible OLED screen. It's breakthroughs like this that can really make life easier for burglars.

French startup UrgoTech has created a wearable padded headband that can read your brainwaves. It aids sleep by measuring your EEG to see if you are right in the head. If you have just spent $600 on a plastic headband to sleep in I think we can already guess.

Modern technology isn't just in the office, it's creeping into all of your other rooms. For $700 you can get a pressure pad to put on your kitchen shelf that will let you know when you have run out of food. I can normally tell if I'm out of food because I get hungry but each to their own.

The best item is the RollBot, invented by the toilet roll company Charmin. If you press a button on an app the RollBot will make its way through your home and deliver you an emergency toilet roll for those moments when someone didn't replace the empty one.

Finally, a technology that is useful. This will end all of those domestic rows we have about forgetting to put the new roll in the bathroom. And it will start domestic rows about someone forgetting to stock up the RollBot cupboard.

No Smoking Work Zones

I am a non-smoker.

That looks like I'm using this column as a dating profile but I mention my smoke-free status to declare a bias about this news story. A company boss in Swindon has given his non-smoking employees an extra four days of annual leave.

As a non-smoker, I like this. I realise that might make some smokers get angry with me but I think I can outrun them.

Don Bryden runs a training company and he said he noticed some smokers take five breaks a day at around ten minutes each. That's nearly an hour off a day. Just under five hours a week. 240 hours across a 48-week year. It's 30 days, so they're still 24 days up on the deal.

I have had this conversation with smoking colleagues (they were colleagues who smoked, I'm not saying they were sexy) and a lot have said it's an addiction and therefore not their fault.

Someone who can't give up the booze doesn't get to stand outside the front door getting their hip flask out for ten minutes. Gamblers don't have paid FOBT breaks. That argument is a little weak.

One smoker once said if I wanted to go and stand outside the office entrance for no reason I could and therefore it's my fault for not taking the option. No I couldn't. I'd look like a right oddball and besides, it smells of smoke out there.

One colleague said smoking made him more productive. If he had to sit there craving a cigarette he'd get less work done. Well, having an afternoon nap would make me more productive but I'm sure regular kips under my desk would be mentioned in my annual review.

It will be interesting to see how this story pans out. Will it be seen as a form of discrimination? Is it OK to give more days off to some members of staff because of their habits? Does that mean we can dock the pay of slow-walkers? (I would be in favour of that too.) Can we take holiday time away from people who spend ages in the toilets? (I'm against that. Don't ask.)

If your company brings in a rule that benefits the non-smokers you could always quit. The job or the habit, but we live in an age of flexible working where employers get in trouble for preferring staff members who have no distractions from work.

My biggest worry is that all this will end with industrial action. If smokers form picket lines, standing outside their place of work instead of being inside doing their jobs, how will we tell the difference?

Big Bad Ben

How will you feel when Brexit happens in silence? For many that should be a good thing. Lots of people have been desperate to get Brexit done and even more people have been begging for a bit of peace and quiet on the issue.

The soundtrack that will be missing is the chiming of Big Ben. The House of Commons decided it wouldn't stump up the extra dosh needed to get the bongs to mark the moment of Brexit. It's because Elizabeth Tower, as it is officially known (called Elizabeth but goes by Ben, how very modern), is currently being repaired.

It would have been £500,000 of taxpayers' money. If the reason you wanted Brexit in the first place was to stop wasting taxpayers' money it seems like a strange way to mark the occasion. It's akin to celebrating Brexit by giving away lots of fish to Norway.

Surely someone has a recording of Big Ben. It's quite famous. Play that out of your phone speaker instead. If you need help with the technology ask a young person on a bus, they seem to be very gifted at using their phones to play things out loud.

Boris Johnson's plan is to crowdfund the money. What I

like about this idea is that he has effectively made Big Ben go private. People accused him of wanting to do that to our health service but it was the clocks he was gunning for all along.

Some people say ringing the bells to celebrate leaving the EU would rub the noses of the 48% who voted to remain in it, although seeing as we have earplug technology we could sort that.

Either way, there's no need to get angry about it. But this issue has made people form two tribes who get mad at each other. Probably about 52% to 48%. Yeah, that rings a bell.

His Royal Bye-ness

They're calling it a constitutional crisis, but they call most things a constitutional crisis these days.

Harry and Meghan's planned retirement has caused more of an argument than any story other than Brexit. Let me show you the way to inner peace on this issue, you can stop caring.

It seems that the people who spent their time complaining that the royals do nothing while taking our money are the ones outraged that the young couple are leaving to do nothing with their own money.

This is where people will start to bring up all of the financial benefits that the Sussexes have received. Yeah, they're royal. Getting more than you deserve is almost the definition of it. They always do well off our backs. I'm just grateful the family in charge lost their right to behead people like us.

Angry defenders of the royals have been bringing up how much money Harry and Meghan have brought to the UK economy. How do we know what proportion of that money was from the people? In France they still get a lot of tourists visiting their palaces and look at what they did to their royals.

There are those who are upset that the way-down-the-line-to-the-throne couple take a lot of flights while telling the rest of us to fly less. Here's my secret weapon to deal with this hypocrisy, I ignore them. Don't listen to people who were born into a fancy family or found fame on TV. Listen to the clever and not the rich and you'll be much happier.

If the anger is still bubbling up inside you ask yourself if you'd want to be royal. I wouldn't. It's a life filled with mostly mundane public appearances and the press spending their time and resources trying to get dirt on you.

Meghan could have been suited to the job. Before she was in the TV show *Suits* she was a glamorous assistant on a TV quiz show where you stand there, smile and make the prize look good. If you swap that prize for a community centre or charity it's the same gig.

Will it really affect your life? If the Duke and Duchess quit without telling me I don't think I would have noticed.

The logic should be simple. If you don't like Meghan you should be happy they're off. If you think all Meghan-haters are bigots you should be happy they're escaping.

Remember, it's not even the biggest scandal to hit the Royal Family in the last few months. Give it a few weeks and I'm sure there will be another.

Artist Formerly Known As Prince

The Duchess of Cornwall visited Prospect Hospice in Swindon recently, but there was no hiding from the fact it wouldn't be the biggest royal story people are talking about. Imagine what she'd have to do to bump Meghan off the front pages. Doing doughnuts in the car park while screaming, "I drive like Daddy-in-law!"

Zara Tindall got a six month ban from driving recently and must have been counting her lucky stars that she did it during Megxit. She avoided a scandal. Even Andrew could be planning a trip to get dough balls in Woking without too much worry.

The biggest story is the departure of Harry and Meghan. It's been announced that they won't receive money for royal duties and won't use their HRH titles.

Like most issues these days, this story has created two opposing groups who disagree passionately and angrily.

It's important to remember that none of this will actually impact our lives. The tabloids will still pursue them.

The odds of people like us getting to meet the royal couple were near zero anyway. If you need a royal for an event they can send plenty of others, they have loads. Duchess of Cornwall, Duke of Cambridge, Earl of Wessex, basically anyone who sounds like a pub.

I wish them the best and look forward to spending less on the monarchy.

For ages the once-royal couple had complained about the treatment they received. Some people said, "If you don't like it, leave."

Harry and Meghan then said they wanted to leave. Some people said, "Oh, I see. You want to have your cake and eat it."

Harry and Meghan then said, "Keep your cake. We'll be fine on the dessert front, thanks". And still people are angry.

It isn't a perfect solution. We're told they won't use their HRH titles. I would have preferred it if they no longer had their HRH titles rather than simply choose to rest them for a while.

Considering yourself a "Highness" but not forcing people to call you it doesn't make you like the rest of us. Quietly thinking you are superior makes you more like a cat.

The new arrangement comes into effect in Spring this year. Imagine what it will be like on March 19th, the last day of Winter. They'll have one last hurrah, when they'll be running around getting people to bow and opening any community centre they can get their hands on.

Don't be angry. Enjoy this news story for what it is. It's a family that lives off the state and they're falling out in public. It's like having The Jeremy Kyle Show back again.

What's In A Name?

The name calling has already started as interest in who will be the next Labour leader heats up, but for Rebecca Long-Bailey the attention is getting a little weird.

People have been trying to find out if she is Rebecca Long-Bailey or Rebecca Long Bailey, without the hyphen. It's important to know. You have to get the details right if you're going to join the millions of other Twitter-users who think they're clever for making the Rebecca Wrong-Daily joke. Or should that be Rebecca Wrong Daily?

Mocking someone for their name is hardly biting satire and I started to feel sorry for Rebecca until I remembered Jeremy Hunt.

The Labour leadership contender's team had told media outlets that her name is officially Long Bailey. Brilliant. Save yourself the trouble of trying to find where the hyphen is on your phone when you want to tweet her.

Hang on. Her Twitter page has her as a Long-Bailey.

The name on Twitter doesn't mean much. In the run up to the last election CCHQ's Twitter name was changed to FactCheckUK, so we know it's not to be trusted. It's the handle that counts, the bit after the @ sign.

In this case she is @RLong_Bailey. An underscore? That's

not helping anyone.

I'm not a fan of double-barrelling names in general. It's OK now but we're storing up trouble. We'll end up in a world of quad-barrelled or octo-barrelled. In fact, spoiler alert, it's $[2^{(n-1)}]$-barrelled names where n is the number of generations.

After just 10 generations that's a 512-barrelled name. It would take hours to fill out any forms.

Thankfully the MP herself cleared the matter up. In an interview Rebecca said, "There actually is a hyphen but I'm not bothered."

That's a healthy attitude. Maybe she won't be affected by the name calling. Or is that name-calling?

Hair Stress

Life can be pretty stressful. A study ranking the most stressful events in life has getting divorced at number two, but number seven on the list is getting married, so at least you had some practice dealing with it.

Scientists now say they may have discovered that stress makes your hair go grey.

Science really is just catching up on things we already knew. I bet there's a team following bears around with a bucket and a map. Spoiler alert: you might want to head to the woods.

The researchers from America and Brazil teamed up to do experiments on mice. They found stem cells controlling skin and hair colour became damaged after intense stress.

Firstly, did they realise that some mice are white already? I hope so.

Secondly, how much stress does a mouse go through? I thought this would explain why if you have faced redundancy or moving house you might start to notice the odd grey strand, but do mice worry about job losses? Does Mr Mouse go home and tell his missus that Bagpuss announced cutbacks and they all have to reapply for their positions?

How can this research help us humans? If you want to keep your glowing and coloured hair, avoid the stress of going near cats?

The stem cells that create hair colour are used up during times of stress. Does this mean the more hair cells you have, the better you will be at dealing with stress?

That's bad news for balding people like myself. Although if you include back hair I might be the most resilient person alive. Yeah, they don't warn you about that in school but as you get older you stop needing Head and Shoulders and start needing Shoulders and Back.

This research raises more questions than it answers. If being stressed makes your hair turn grey just how bad was Phillip Schofield's life? Was Gordon The Gopher that hard to work with?

As ever, I think this piece of science news can help me make my first million. I'm going to make money selling grey hair dye. Not hair dye for grey hair, dye to turn your hair grey.

Everyone loves to claim that they're really busy and stressed these days. If you ask how someone has been they will tell you how much of a challenge they're up against. With Steve N Allen's new improved Greycian 2000 you can look like you're so stressed your stem cells ran out years ago.

Taxing

January 31st means a lot of us are about to get poorer.

Now you are worried that I have turned into a Remoaner and I'll start saying the inscription on the new 50 pence piece might as well read, "Ner ner ner ner ner." That's not it. I am referring to the self-assessment deadline. They say tax doesn't have to be taxing and yet, as January draws to a close, it is.

To make things worse a list of Britain's top taxpayers has been released. That means, not only are these people rich, they also have their tax return in already. That's two reasons to be jealous.

We could analyse the kind of people on the list, for example at the top we find Denise Coates, founder of Bet365. Some people say there are issues with a person making that much money from people losing bets but for every Bet365 there could be another betting company that folded. Someone may have launched Bet366, which only makes money in a leap year. The point is, she gambled and won.

I think the more interesting fact about Britain's top taxpayers list is that it is not the same as the rich list. It feels deep down that those two lists should be similar.

One of the reasons the lists don't match is that people do what they can to pay less tax. That makes sense, we all try to cut costs. If you can afford the kind of accountant that is good at reducing that bill you'll pay less.

It's not the same as all of the other outgoings though. People will often boast about how much they give to charity. Why don't we view paying tax in the same way?

When we hear someone brag about how tax efficient they are why don't we translate that in our heads as, "I am doing all I can to make sure I don't help the UK?"

A place on the taxpayers list should be a thing of pride. It shows you have achieved greatness and you haven't tried to move your bank accounts to an unpopulated island somewhere.

There are people who, when they hear about the floating

Great Pacific Garbage Patch that's now three times the size of France, think about trying to register a company there.

Do you want your tax pounds to help your fellow citizens or help some penguins somewhere?

Even though I believe that paying tax is good, I do it too. I have a great system in place to make sure I don't pay a lot of tax. I am not that successful. It works a treat.

2 FEBRUARY

Down The Pub

I often write these columns while sitting in a pub. You can tell which ones because they end with many typos and me saying, "I love you, you're my best friend."

One pub chain has brought in a new rule which has upset some parents but may have made it easier for people like me who can't afford an office.

Wetherspoons has told parents that if they are in the pub with their children and they are having alcoholic drinks they can only have a maximum of two.

At first I thought that sounded like the one-child policy of China in the 80s but then I realised they meant only two drinks.

I'm sure most parents look after their offspring while out drinking but a few of them have a great time while letting the rest of the world be their crèche.

Why is it the age at which children like to run around is the age when they have reached the height of most tables? No wonder the parents need a drink; watching those little heads dash round near solid oak is terrifying.

Before we break this down into an argument about whether the rule is good let's ask this question, who is going out for three or more drinks with their toddlers? They are hardly able to walk and unable to communicate properly, and they're in charge of their toddlers.

I know the children won't be drinking and seeing as kids these days have those little electric mini-cars they could be the designated driver.

This was never a problem when I was growing up. The bars in pubs were adult places that we weren't allowed into. On those rare occasions that I could glimpse through a slowly-closing door, I saw a bar that looked like the helm of a spaceship with all of those pumps and optics. Granted it was a spaceship that had a sheet of peanuts slowly revealing a Page 3 girl, but who knows what things will be like in space. There's no gravity up there, so that explains part of the look.

Whether you think this rule is positive or not we can all agree it is unworkable. There is nothing to stop someone popping into one pub to have a couple with their family and then walking to the next and doing the same. They could spend all day doing the family pub crawl.

Look on the bright side, at least it will increase their step count.

Oh, and I love you and you're my beast freindd.

Ban The Car

When we knew we were getting a Boris Johnson government I bet you didn't expect more things to be banned, but we could soon see a ban on petrol and diesel cars.

From 2035 the sale of such items could be outlawed and it

will be hard to do that sale under the counter. Dodgy blokes in pubs can't really have a petrol car hidden in their long coat.

The Government had previously said those vehicles would be banned from 2040, but it brought the date forward by five years. After that point it will be electric or maybe hydrogen cars only. Can you imagine what an episode of Top Gear will be like in the year 2037? Of course you can't, it won't be on. There won't be a BBC by then.

This is bad news for petrolheads. You'll only be allowed to be an electric head, and that sounds like your hair is standing up while you're touching a Van de Graaff generator.

It'll be like when they had to play the recording of Big Ben to mark Brexit because the real one couldn't make a sound. You'll have to have a CD of car sound effects if you want to rev your engine. But don't play it too loudly, you'll run your car battery down.

Why are they doing this? To save the planet, which is where most of us live.

I know change can be difficult for some. Electric cars sound futuristic. Don't worry, they don't have really long extension cables trailing behind them. You can still wash an electric car without having to put it in a bag of rice overnight to dry off the circuits.

We will miss the old cars but it means some things will improve. No more going to the petrol station to fill up, which means you won't have the nightmare of seeing the cost tick up from £19.98 to £19.99 and then £20.02. Darn it! I'm sure they do that on purpose to get another tenner out of people like me.

We will have a quiet life without motors roaring. We will breathe cleaner air without exhaust fumes being pumped out so close to the pavements. And most importantly we can feel less guilty about our lifestyle when we are living in a country that is carbon-neutral.

Switching from burning petrol to using lithium batteries will mean we don't pollute the planet as much.

It's the countries that are manufacturing those batteries for us that will be messing up the Earth. Tut.

Trust The Police

Do you trust the police? I don't mean in a way you'd see in a film with you saying, "We can't take this to the police, we don't know how high up this alien invasion goes." I mean it in the simple sense of trusting them to solve your crimes.

Matt Parr, HM Inspector of Constabulary, has said the failure of the police to investigate high-volume crimes like car thefts, assaults and burglaries was having a "corrosive" effect on the public's trust in the police.

Many of us have been in the situation where you are the victim of a crime but you wonder if it's worth your while reporting it. If no one investigates it and all you are is recorded as a statistic it feels like you're taking part in a market research survey for the police and little more.

It can't be the police themselves. We often hear of an off-duty officer stopping a terrorist on the streets of London. Those people earn the public's respect and trust. It must be the system.

Even the extra 20,000 officers promised will only take the system's staffing levels back to the numbers they were in 2010 when we had far less cyber crime and online bullying to investigate.

I have had both in my time. I have been the victim of online abuse and I had my car broken into a few roads away from Hackney Downs station. I know which I'd rather be protected from in the future.

In case you wondered, they didn't nick the car but they got away with the bag that was on the back seat. All it had in it was five pairs of pants. I'd like to think in this case the criminals got exactly what they deserved.

Save The NHS

There's a place in my heart for the Great Western Hospital. It has been there when I needed it. That may be why I have a natural urge to defend our NHS when I hear that someone is coming for it.

It's not the person you think I'm going to talk about. This is not a Donald Trump column. I don't even know if America would be bad at running the NHS. They chlorinate their chicken so they might manage to clean a ward or two.

I'm talking about the actress Gwyneth Paltrow. She has a website and health brand called Goop. It sells things like a £40 tub of salt to put on your hair which is basically seasoning yourself in case you meet a cannibal. She famously sells a candle that smells like she smuggled it into prison, if I can put it that way.

There are loads of health and well-being items on her site. For £26 you can actually buy psychic vampire repellent. Save yourself £26 and just think about buying it. The psychic vampires will know you're planning it and they won't bother.

On her site they say the psychic vampire repellent is an "essential oil blend of lavender, rosemary, and juniper". Well, garlic gets rid of standard vampires so why not?

NHS boss Sir Simon Stevens said that firms like Goop were offering dubious wellness products and "dodgy procedures". Gwyneth has defended her brand. She said that Sir Stevens' claims were BS, you know, something that comes out of a bull.

I think she means that as an insult, but there is a chance that she thinks stuff that comes from a bull is actually a really great face mask and it'll cost you £93.

She refuted the accusation that her brand is 'pseudo-scientific'. On that issue we agree. Talking about getting rid of vampires by using a different garnish isn't scientific in the slightest. It's barely pseudo-cooking.

Gwyneth said that such criticism is "clickbait". She said, "People are able to criticise us now in opportunistic ways. It's a cheap and easy way to try and drive traffic to these sites."

I'm not sure that the NHS is trying to get more people to its website. It's the one business that has a better time the fewer people use it.

But Gwyneth might be right about me. Maybe my sarcastic joke-making about Goop may be nothing more than cheap and easy attention-seeking.

Quick! Open a jar of vanilla, sandalwood and sage. That'll get rid of me.

A Bridge Too Far

We understand the value of a bridge. If you've ever had to waste your time queuing up to get over the QEII Bridge you would have felt the value of it when the fine came if you forgot to pay.

The new bridge that's being talked about won't really help us, it will be on the other side of the country connecting Scotland to Northern Ireland. No. 10 has said that work is under way "by a range of government officials".

Let's hope they don't put anyone who has worked on HS2 in charge of the bridge because the cost will go up so quickly there'll be a statement along the lines of, "We predict this project will come in at £3.5billion. And that £15billion is money well spent. For that £35billion we will boost the economy, so we can all agree the cost of £49billion isn't too much. £80billion!"

Another challenge is that it would be built over millions of tons of dumped munitions but I am someone who likes to turn a negative into a positive. It will make sure you pay attention to your driving as you go across. No one will want to risk dropping off the side.

The bigger worry is timing. While the idea of a Scotland-Northern Ireland bridge may be appealing to some, there's a chance that by the time it's finished it will be a bridge between the Republic of Scotland and the United Isle of Ireland.

Some have said that Boris Johnson's bridge is similar to Donald Trump's wall. I suppose a wall is basically a bridge on its side but I think the big difference is that when Scotland gets this bridge it actually will have been paid for by those south of the border.

Name That Storm

The recent weather shows how powerful the planet is. My heart goes out to anyone who has been affected by the storms. I drive a small car and it felt like I was using all the lanes of the M4 at once when the winds were gusting.

I know other parts of the UK had it worse but we saw some road closures in Wroughton where flooding was a problem. The fire service warned people not to drive through flood water and I am always surprised that we need that advice. You'd think it would be obvious but so many people try it.

I blame the Bond films of the 1970s. We got so used to

seeing Roger Moore in an amphibious Lotus Esprit S1 we all think we can drive in water.

There's another reason we don't respect the power of these storms, the names. In the last few years we have adopted the American system of giving names to storms and I think it messes with the psychology of the situation.

If you call anything Dennis you make it less frightening. Even Dennis the Menace was only scary because of his middle and surname. We've all known a Dennis. Probably a quiet chap you see down the local. Even his drink of choice is a pint of mild.

If you hear that a big storm is coming this weekend you'd batten down the hatches. If you hear that Dennis is coming this weekend you'd make sure you have enough milk in.

Before Dennis we had Storm Ciara. Why give a storm a name that many didn't know how to pronounce? What if you needed to shout in an emergency, "Get inside, here's Storm See... Cha... Ki... oh, forget it!"

A study found that people are less afraid of storms that are named after women. Not only does that show the everyday sexism at play it also puts people at risk. If the powers that be name a storm something like Daisy or Winifred more people will risk going out in it.

If they insist on naming storms, they should be forced to name the bad ones things like Cruella or Maleficent. Even a basic rule like, "If the storm's name sounds like it could have been one of ITV's Gladiators don't go out," could keep us safe.

The worst case scenario would be naming a storm Alexa. Not only would it cause flooding and travel problems it would also crash the Internet.

I preferred the old days when we didn't use names. So be careful out there. There could be gales.

Save The BBC

When was the last time you used the BBC? You could be an EastEnders fan. Maybe you enjoyed Fleabag. Maybe you have the news app that makes you think you've got a message from a friend but then you find out it's just a war being declared. Maybe you downloaded my BBC podcast "Steve N Allen's Week". Hint!

If it wasn't for the BBC I'd have to be back on radio around here, so you've already benefitted from it.

New figures show there are 200,000 fewer licences this year. If we bear in mind there are more people in the UK, what's going on?

Maybe it's easier to dodge these days. We used to live in fear of the detector vans that could somehow tell if you were watching TV. The more I think about it the more I realise it probably involved looking in through your window and seeing the glow on your face.

If the detector people turned up and you didn't have a licence you had to go into panic mode. You'd move the TV out into the garden and try to convince the officials you pointed all your furniture at that empty table because you liked the dust patterns on it.

That may have been why rock stars threw TVs out of hotel windows. They'd get a knock on the door from room service, in their drug-addled state think it was the detector people and get rid of the evidence. Thanks to the iPlayer, if you want to hide the fact you were just watching TV you have to press alt-tab.

Don't worry about the BBC being under-funded. You may have noticed they have instituted an advanced technological solution on their digital platform. Before it lets you watch a show on the iPlayer it asks, "Do you have a licence?"

Yeah, foolproof.

Spending Forecast

When I was walking with my father on a trip to Sutton Lawn the force of the recent storms was apparent. I wouldn't fancy being one of those trees trying to stand up in that.

My Dad was shouting, "Ay up, int it code?" to anyone walking by, which I find is a good test to work out if they're locals or not.

This odd weather should be easier to predict in the future now that the Met Office is to be given £1billion to build a supercomputer. That seems like a lot of money for a computer, or it seems about right if you want to buy an Apple one.

They claim that this new beast will be six times more powerful than the supercomputer they currently use. Even so, I bet it hangs for ages when it gets to 99% on the Windows update.

At the moment we have the technology to predict weather in 1.5km squares but the new system will make that 100m squares. They'll be able to predict the weather on a street-by-street basis. The weather forecast will take ages doing it that way. ITV will be half an hour late for Coronation Street and the weather person will have only done the Carsic Estate.

I am all for technological advancement but in my experience the weather on one street is pretty much the same as the weather on the next. And if I ever find myself one street away from nice weather, I can walk over there.

The problem is that £1billion would make a big difference helping those who have flooding in their homes when the extreme weather hits. A computer will let them know it's coming earlier but it won't stop the flood. It means people can move things on to higher shelves with less of a rush.

A new computer will give better weather warnings but people don't listen to them. Michael Fish messed up in the 80s and now we don't believe anything they say. All that money spent telling us bad weather is on the way and people will still stay in their home.

My worry is that we won't spend the money stopping floods, we will spend it all on a fancy computer and then after a really bad storm hits there will be a chance that the flood will damage the Met Office computer. And then what?

All we can hope is that the Met Office computer stores all its data in the cloud.

Storms vs. Leisure

I used to love a stroll around Hackney Downs. The fresh air, the greenery, the patches on the picnic tables where people have used disposable barbecues and it's melted a perfect rectangle in the plastic, all of that would brighten my day.

This year has changed things though. It seems like every weekend has had a storm. The weather has been so intense it made a walk on the Downs feel like an extreme sport.

On the plus side the winds would have been too strong to light a barbecue so at least the plastic picnic tables were spared.

If the weather is going to keep getting worse we can expect to hear more from Extinction Rebellion. Recently they were up in Cambridge upsetting the university by digging up their lawns. It was nice to know they weren't messing up our public transport in London but if they dig up our grassy areas where am I going to have my disposable barbecue now?

If we want to have our leisure time indoors there was good news in the form of plans for a £30million redevelopment of Lee Valley Ice Centre. It will be perfect for me for those six weeks of the year when Dancing On Ice is on TV and I become an expert on ice skating. It's months before the two weeks in the summer when I'm a tennis expert, and the weekend in May when I know about voting patterns across Europe.

Some people think that £30million is a lot of money. I am here to help. We can cut the cost of any redevelopment plan by simply claiming that the owners are going to do something bad for the environment and then Extinction Rebellion will turn up and dig up anything we need them to.

Studios

We could be in for a new development. I'm not talking about some housing project, we could be getting our own film studio.

Admittedly it feels like the housing crisis is a bigger one than the shortage of film studios, but it is a real issue.

When we started on The Mash Report we were in The London Studios near Waterloo. Sadly that closed in 2018. It was a shame because it was on the Jubilee line and I am not famous enough to get a car provided for me.

While working at The London Studios, once I got in a lift with Stacey Solomon. They say never meet your heroes, so being in the same building as the Loose Women was safe.

After that we moved to Pinewood, a place with such heritage. There's a slim chance that I used a bathroom Sir Alec Guinness had been in.

The problem with Pinewood is that it is in the middle of nowhere. There are no train stations near it. You can't even get a direct bus from Slough train station. I am not sure how Sir Alec coped with having to change buses. Did he have the right money or did he pull the old, "These are not the tickets you're looking for," trick?

For the next series we are moving to Elstree. That's where EastEnders is filmed. It's a long journey on a Thameslink train to get to a pretend version of East London.

That's why I want Barking to have a studio. The site where the studio could be is right by Dagenham East tube station. Not only will it be useful for all the productions displaced by the closure of The London Studios but it also will be able to attract great films and TV shows and, more importantly, I'd get to work quicker.

The New 20

As soon as a new version of a coin or note is released we hear that some of them are worth more than their face value. There were many news stories after the new 50p and £1 coin came out saying if you had a certain number on it, it would be worth twice what it should be. I don't spend that long looking at my pocket change, which is why I have often tried to pay for things with yellow chips from the car park and the odd embarrassing hair.

Now there's an eBay seller from Swindon who was looking to sell a new £20 for £25. It almost makes sense. If the old, tatty paper-based notes are worth £20 it seems fitting that the new, improved ones will cost more.

The old notes have a picture on them of Adam Smith. Who wants a headshot of an economist? The new ones feature JMW Turner and trendy people have pictures of artists, so that adds value.

Not everything about the new note is good. While the old ones are made of paper these new ones are polymer notes. I thought we were trying to stop using plastics. I have been carrying a bag for life around like an idiot while the Bank of England has been making a twenty that we can't throw in the ocean.

They say it's a harder note to counterfeit, which means the eBay seller should get better feedback. I'm glad something has been done. The old note was apparently easy to copy. I hope that's why every time I tried to spend one the shopkeeper would hold it under a UV lamp. If it didn't happen to you too I must have a very untrustworthy face, which as you can see from my picture on this column, is a strong possibility.

They can go back to using those UV lights to dry their nail varnish.

New security features include raised dots, a purple foil patch, a hologram and a see-through window. That last one is also useful if you're spying on someone. You can pretend you're looking at your money but actually you're keeping an eye on your target.

The new £20 may be worth £25 but it won't last long. I've seen Antiques Roadshow and it's always the out of date denominations that are worth more. Don't buy the new note from that Swindon eBayer, track me down online and I'll sell you the notes and coins I have for twice their value. It'll pay off in the long run.

Although there is a chance I'll send you a yellow chip from the car park and a hair.

Another New Note

When did you last check your mobile phone? For some the answer will be, "Halfway through reading that last sentence, Steve." We're phone addicts these days. I'd give out the number for the helpline but that would make things worse.

New data has come out ranking the areas of London with the most phone thefts. I'm not sure what we are meant to do with this information. Are we meant to get on a train and go to Bexley to make a call because you're less likely to get mugged for it there?

The data tells us that journey would be fraught with phone danger. You'd get on the train and head through Redbridge, which is twelfth on the list for where you're most likely to get your phone nicked. 4,538 mobiles were stolen there over the three-year period.

It gets worse. As your train stops at Stratford you're in Newham which was seventh on the list with 9,805 thefts. Why even bother putting up phone masts?

Before you feel bad about our level of telephone larceny get ready for the Tube bit of the journey. Circle Line from Liverpool Street to Monument so you can walk to London Bridge for the train to Bexley? Don't stay on by accident. The top of the phone theft league was Westminster with 33,330 phones being tea-leafed.

That's the home of Parliament. No wonder they keep losing top secret documents if they can't even keep hold of their phones.

The problem is we're phone zombies who walk around holding our phones out. We're doing the pickpocketers' work for them.

Don't get me wrong, I enjoy seeing someone walk into a lamp post as much as anyone but if these stats make us put our phones away and pay attention to the real world in front of us, rob away, rob away!

The Truth About BMW Drivers

I travel quite a bit for work and it has always been a source of regional pride for me that our roads in Nottinghamshire are safe.

If I go to cross on a zebra crossing on Outram Street I am

pretty sure the car will stop, the driver and I will exchange a nod of our respective heads communicating our mutual respect, and we'll go about our day.

If I am filming down in London and I need to go over a zebra crossing it's like an extreme sport. People speed up. If it wasn't for the training I had by playing Horace Goes Skiing on the ZX Spectrum growing up I'd never get to the job.

I thought it was a sign that we are nicer up here than the people in London but new research has found it might be something else.

Drivers of expensive cars are more dangerous to pedestrians. A study found the chances of a car stopping at a zebra crossing falls by three per cent for every £800 rise in their vehicle's value.

What I thought was a sign of nicer people up here may actually be a sign of fancier cars down there.

The research backs up the old stereotypes of certain drivers. I don't know if BMWs have their indicators disconnected before they are allowed on the motorway. I don't know if the people who drive them are choosing not to indicate because they want to cut down their carbon-footprint, but they have the reputation for being stoic in their signalling.

Does this fit with the data, the more expensive the car the less considerate the driver?

Let's test the opposite case. If you see some old chap in an X-reg Honda they seem to leave their indicators on all the time. Very considerate. Maybe there's something in this.

Maybe people driving flashier cars are busy people so they don't want to stop to let you cross, whereas people in cheaper cars can't afford to do much accelerating, what with the price of petrol these days, so they let you go.

Other studies have found a greater incidence of sociopathy in top business people and they drive nice motors. I have solved the mystery.

If more expensive cars make drivers more dangerous, we should cut VAT on cars and make the roads 20 per cent safer. They could add that to the Budget on March 11th unless Rishi Sunak doesn't care about safety.

And yes, I may be looking for a car at the moment, but that's just a coincidence.

3 MARCH

Baby Boris

Congratulations to Prime Minister Boris Johnson and Carrie Symonds who have announced they are expecting a baby. They say it's due in the early summer, but if previous form is anything to go by that will probably move to autumn or winter and come in a few billion over budget.

We're all happy for them, especially her, with a name like Carrie she seems suited to being pregnant. We can all imagine her looking adoringly at that podgy little face, hearing those sounds that aren't talking, they're just sweet little nonsensical noises, realising that he is going to be the father of her child.

It's nice to know you can be Prime Minister and still find time to get up to fun with your partner. Maybe their former neighbours were wrong; that shouting and screaming wasn't a row.

Boris and Carrie have also announced their engagement, which makes Mr Johnson the first Prime Minister to get divorced and then married again while in office. Who knows, if the Labour party doesn't sort itself out, he may be the first Prime Minister to get divorced, married, divorced again, married once more and get a bus pass.

These days everything is political so there are many who think the timing of this happy news is a little suspicious. Some think this is coming out now to bury the story about Priti Patel being accused of bullying.

While the timing of announcement could have helped to push the Home Secretary off the front pages I don't think the actual pregnancy could have been. It's been a long time since I was taught about the birds and the bees at school but it takes a little time. And I don't mean ten minutes if you include the five minutes of pleading. You can't rush these things. I know Dominic Cummings is said to be a genius but even he can't change biology.

I just had another lovely thought of Carrie looking at that cute bald head, hearing all that crying, and realising that man is the advisor to the father of her child.

By having a child with Boris Johnson, Carrie joins an elite club with an undisclosed number of members. In the past he has refused to answer interviewers' questions about the number of children he has. Many say he has a good point. Why should we know the details of someone's private life? After all, having children is one of the most private things.

But if that's your point of view, why would you break the news about having another child? Maybe someone bullied him into it. We couldn't possibly say.

Covid-19 for Introverts

While the Covid-19 situation is worrying we shouldn't panic. The panic could be worse than the disease. We're already hearing about a potential shortage of toilet roll. They say society is two meals away from anarchy. Well, we all know what happens to those meals a few hours later, so let's not make everything worse.

As an introvert, some of the advice we're being told is really good to hear. That may shock some people. No one thinks that stand-up comedians could be introverted but I did a test, online, at home, on my own – the signs were there.

We're being told to avoid hugging. Yes please. I have struggled with that for years. People you've only met once before greet you with open arms like you're a long lost sibling. I feel like a cat in a Pepé Le Pew cartoon struggling to get out of their arms.

We are also told to avoid leaving the house to go to places with lots of people. That sounds like my ideal weekend.

Some people are also avoiding anyone who has recently come back from Tenerife. I already do, but mainly for fear of having to sit through the holiday photos.

Not all of the advice is good for us introverts. I read that we should avoid touching things in public that ill people may have touched. Three hours I was at that pelican crossing. I suppose I could have asked someone to help but, you know, I'm an introvert.

The advice I read said, "Do not use your finger to press buttons." I cannot tell you what I used instead but I can tell you I am now not legally allowed within 50 yards of that ATM.

I had to change my PIN number to 7899. I couldn't reach the higher up rows.

It's great that we are focussing on hygiene. We're washing our hands and doing all the different types of rubs, like we're the sign language guy on BBC Learning Zone. We're standing in the work bathrooms singing Happy Birthday, which keeps us clean, and if someone walks in and it is their birthday they'll think we remembered.

It's great that we're being careful about passing on germs and tutting when we see someone cough or sneeze without covering their mouths.

I only hope that when COVID goes the way of SARS, MERS, bird and swine flu, we still keep up with these basic manners that we should never have forgotten in the first place.

Caught Short

In the face of a crisis we should help one another rather than selfishly panic buy.

Covid-19 is a genuine worry but panicking only ever makes things worse. People are panic buying so much toilet paper the UK could be facing a shortage. There is no problem that isn't made worse by the lack of toilet paper when you need it.

We're not the only nation to face the terrifying prospect of the disappointing penguin-waddle to the cupboard. Australia has already seen shelves stripped bare of two-ply. Even though there's no reason to think they'd run out as most of their supplies are made locally in the country.

It happened in Hong Kong too where there were reports of armed robbers taking toilet rolls. A scary ordeal to go through, but there's no point in getting too frightened as you don't have any loo roll any more.

Will we have to see security-tagged Charmin? Andrex with dye packs installed so if the robbers try to open the package they become traceable? Izal toilet paper is already traceable, as you can use it to trace pictures more successfully than use it for its intended purpose.

I don't know how these panic buyers do it. I feel very self-conscious if I buy too many toilet rolls at once, almost like I have to explain the purchase. I once went to the corner shop and bought milk and a 9-pack and I had to fight the urge to say, "Lactose intolerance," as I handed over the money.

Some toilet rolls are selling online for hundreds of dollars. This is where I can help. You can get my paperback books online for a couple of quid. Use those. It'll save you money and I'll move up the Amazon charts. I don't mind, I've had worse reviews.

Panic Buying Again

When I lived near the Tawny Owl pub I had a plan. If anything bad happened to the world, like a zombie apocalypse or computers turn on us, I'd walk to the big Asda like the guy in The War of the Worlds and live off all the things in there. I now realise my plan was flawed. Our supermarkets are the first things to get emptied when panic happens.

Panic buying tells us a lot about our priorities. When we were told there was a spread of a respiratory disease the first thing we had a run on was toilet roll. It shows it's the one thing we really don't want to live without. Anyone who didn't list loo roll as the thing they'd take with them on Desert Island Discs was clearly lying.

The next wave of panic buying was soap. At first I thought this was because people had taken the advice about hand washing but I have a terrible feeling it's because the one thing you need when you no longer have toilet roll is soap.

Why didn't people have soap in the house already? How many people weren't washing their hands at all before they were told to by Matt Hancock?

I have also seen photographs on Twitter of some supermarkets stripped bare of biscuits. I understand that. If there is a chance I may be forced to self-isolate at home for two weeks I will go willingly as long as I have plenty of biscuits in.

There's a serious side to panic buying. It shows that we are losing a sense of community. Panic buying is selfish. It's "me first" regardless of need.

In America there were cases of people stockpiling face masks, which experts say don't really help you avoid catching Covid-19, but that meant there were none available for the medical staff who needed to wear them.

If you have enough toilet roll and soap to see you through, but you want to make sure you buy all you can get, you're leaving others with none.

People with cash to spare and big cars can get mountains of bathroom products. The people who have to live from hand-to-mouth (well, not mouth in this case, but you get the point) will be left with none.

We'll end up in a different HG Wells story. In The Time Machine, society has broken down into two groups. We could end up with those with toilet roll, and those without. And that's an uprising that will be messy.

So don't panic buy. The worst thing we could run out of now is common sense.

Hug A Princess

The Duke and Duchess of Sussex have made their last public appearance as working members of the Royal Family. The Royal Family is just that little bit smaller now. So, do we just wait for the rebate? Surely they can't cost tax payers as much now, because they're smaller. If anyone needs me I'll be holding my breath.

There's one person who might be happy they've quit, Aker Okoye the young Dagenham student at the school

Meghan went to on International Women's Day. He hit the headlines when he said, "She's beautiful, innit?"

To the more mature reader, I should point out "innit" is just something that young people say. He's not actually saying, "She's beautiful in it." He's not complimenting her coat. He was saying, "She is beautiful, isn't she?"

That's right, the first thing he said about her was to comment on her beauty, on International Women's Day. It's a good job people found him cute or he would have been #MeToo'd at record speed.

He also hugged Meghan. We are living in a time when we're told to avoid physical contact to halt the spread of coronavirus and he's going in for a hug.

It was odd to see because we are so used to the rule, you don't touch the royals but the royals can touch you, and if you do touch them the bouncers will throw you out, and the drinks in that place are overpriced anyway. Sorry, I was thinking of someone else there.

I presumed you weren't allowed to touch the Queen in case you had cheap shoes on and had built up some static.

Aker is lucky. He could have been sent to the tower for hugging a royal. But Meghan isn't royal any more. Well done Aker. Timing, innit?

Do Your Home Work

Coronavirus has impacted all of our lives. Not too long ago, most of us couldn't wait to get home, kick off our shoes and have a nice glass of wine. These days all we want is to get home, wash our hands and give our faces a darn good touch.

I had no idea I enjoyed touching my face so much. I don't know why it feels so good. I'd give it some thought but that would lead to chin stroking and that'll be outlawed soon.

In fact I have started to boycott KFC because of the fears of finger licking.

All of us will see some changes in our day-to-day lives and if that can help this pandemic then we should be happy to sacrifice some things.

Our Chancellor Rishi Sunak said of the Covid-19 crisis, "We will get through this together," which rather makes it look like he doesn't understand what self-isolating is.

If you are working from home because of this virus, let me help. As a freelance writer I have worked from home for many years. There are some simple things you can do to make it easier.

Make home feel like a day in the office. Getting dressed will feel unnecessary but if you sit around in your PJs all day it puts you in the mindset to watch daytime TV.

As a bare minimum you should put smart clothes on your top half. You'll be in a mood to work and you'll look passable on a Skype call as long as you don't stand up to reach for something.

Another big problem when you are at home is you own everything in the nearest fridge and it can be tempting to pop to it for regular snacks.

Make your fridge more like one you'd find in an office. Spill some milk in it now. By the time the coronavirus infection rate peaks in 10 to 14 weeks' time, your fridge will have the cheesy whiff of an office fridge and it will put you off eating every time you open the door.

Don't let people know you're working from home. If they know they will treat you as available to help. You'll be asked to nip to the shops, sign for post, do their bidding. They think, "You've been at home all day, why couldn't you help," but you're at work.

Go and hide in the loft so no one can get to you.

If you really want working at home to feel like going into the office take an hour or so every morning and evening to go and sit in the car and swear at people.

Don't Let Them Profit

I have been trying to think of ways to use a newspaper column to make things better. We are all going to struggle during the coronavirus crisis but we need to find ways to help each other.

I like that I get to write to you on a regular basis, but I want to do more than that. You probably have enough messages from the CEOs of every company you have ever shopped with or logged onto the free wifi of.

I want to use this space over the coming months to share some positive messages. Let's start with this: We can pull together and not buy anything from anyone profiteering during this crisis.

I have seen pictures on social media of people who went to the shops and filled their cars with hand sanitiser and toilet paper and are now trying to flog it online.

I think eBay and Amazon should shut them down. If they don't, we should make a pact not to buy anything from people like that. Leave them with a living room filled with a hundredweight of Andrex and no hope of shifting it. When their friends visit it will look like they have some kind of stomach trouble.

Videos have appeared online of some shopkeepers selling loo roll for £10. I understand the rules of supply and demand, but it is wrong to exploit someone's desperation.

There are 200 sheets per roll, so that's 5p per sheet. Do they know what I'm going to do with it? That's too rich for me.

If you find a shop selling loo roll at extortionate prices

you could always try this. Take it to the checkout, let them scan it, when they ask for you to pay by card you could get your PIN wrong a few times. The cashier will have to void the sale and hand you the receipt and the slip of paper that shows the card was declined. Take those two bits of paper and say, "It's OK, I'll use this instead."

Exponential Growth

Science is helping the coronavirus situation, and it can make you feel better too.

There are the obvious ways science helps, like Dyson making ventilators for the NHS. I hope they're not overpowered like their hand driers. If they are they could inflate people like frogs' throats. People would be rasping round hospitals like a balloon you've let go of.

Science can also make us feel better. We are basically under house arrest because some selfish people went to the seaside one weekend. They didn't take the advice and it feels like we're all being punished for it.

We're locked in and let out to exercise once a day. It's basically prison rules. If I do some crimes in the future I hope they count this as time served off my sentence.

The logic that makes us feel like we have been bad can be used to make us feel better. It's going to get technical but here goes.

Before I did comedy I used to be a scientist. I was recently asked on radio to explain exponential growth, which is how viruses spread.

Imagine you're in a room and once a day you go out and fetch someone to join you. I realise that could be hard to imagine because we're all forgetting what it feels like to go out.

If you fetched a person each day for ten days, at the end

there'd be you and ten people. I've played stand-up gigs like that. Maybe I should have stuck with science. That's linear growth.

What if every person you brought back with you could also fetch someone? You'd fetch someone making two in the room. You two would get two more, making four. Then eight, then 16. Ten days in and there would be 1,024 people in that room. You'd really have to label things in the fridge. And the arguments over the remote control would take ages.

That's exponential growth.

With coronavirus they say you're likely to spread it to three people. In our example, that's like each person leaving the room and bringing back two people, not one.

In that case, ten days later, it's 59,049 people in that room and your landlord should be investigated.

With a mortality rate of 2 per cent, it's 1,180 people who would die.

But turn that around. If you stay in you're saving the lives of more than a thousand people. You are sparing countless more the experience of going into hospital to be inflated on a Dyson ventilator. You're doing that. If that doesn't make you a hero, I don't know what does.

On The Run

Why are people still going out?

When this all started we were advised not to go to pubs but people still went so pubs were closed. We were advised to stay in but people had a nice day out at various beaches.

Some people clearly think, "If everyone else sticks to the rules I don't have to." The problem with that is if everyone thinks it, no one sticks to the rules.

Thanks to people with that attitude we had strict rules imposed and yet still we hear of people breaking the new guidelines. So much so that in one lagoon in the Midlands the police have added black dye to put people off going to see it.

That won't work. I don't have any interest in seeing your average lagoon at the best of times but if you tell me you've added food colouring to make it look like the alien that kills Tasha Yar in Star Trek: The Next Generation I fancy taking a selfie with it.

If you don't stay in you are putting other people's lives at risk. That should be enough of a reason, but if it isn't, try this one. By going out you are making the pedants look like they are in the right.

Some police forces have said they have received lots of calls from people reporting their neighbours for taking more than one run a day.

You know the type. They are the people who will report you to the council if your bin lid won't shut. They'll count how many items you have in your basket as you queue for the ten items or less checkout. You can tell if you live with one of these. If they find a fork that's been washed but still has a little mark on it, they won't simply wash it again, they will spend more energy walking from the kitchen with it just to show you what you did wrong.

By leaving your home when you are not meant to you are making these people right.

Reporting a neighbour for a second run seems like a sneaky move. If they end up in prison for it they'll feel hard done by. They may feel so hard done by they'll try to escape. If they end up "on the run" they will have got what they wanted.

But if we stick to the rules we will take the power away from the curtain-twitchers. I know that shouldn't be the best motivation to do the right thing but it will feel good.

If you want to go for a second run, do it tomorrow.

4 APRIL

Red Card Birthday Cards

If the many graphs we are shown during Government Covid-19 briefings are anything to go by, we are being successful with our social distancing efforts.

It's no time to relax but we can take some credit that we are saving lives. It also means that we, the people, might be showing better judgement than some of the folks enforcing these rules.

There were claims that some shoppers were told off for buying birthday cards during the lockdown because they aren't essential.

We haven't had clear guidance on what is and isn't essential. If you look at the Waitrose definition for its "essentials range" you'd have to include things like vermicelli nests and artichoke hearts, both of which I have made it to this age without.

Anyone who thinks a birthday card isn't essential has clearly never forgotten to give one to their other half before. You'd never hear the end of it and it's not like you can leave the house to get away from the mood it would cause.

For the rest of the world 2020 will be remembered as the year of the coronavirus. For you it would be called, "The year you forgot all about me."

If you're leaving the house just to buy a card you should plan better, but if you're shopping you should be allowed to buy anything that shop sells. If we are going to judge the essentiality of individual items the middle aisle in Aldi might as well be cordoned off.

In the past I have seen those middle aisles sell things like scuba gear, power tools and noise-cancelling headphones. Although they could be considered essential if you haven't bought your partner a birthday card and you need something to block out their response.

I think birthday cards should be allowed as long as you don't lick the envelope. In general, don't lick any of the items you've been shopping for before you give them to people. That's such basic advice they didn't even list it on the Government sites.

Birthday gifts, on the other hand, aren't essential. It's understandable that you couldn't get to normal shops to get a gift. I imagine big shops will be empty of wrapping paper. It's the next aisle I'd go to if they were out of toilet roll.

Don't put money in the card as a gift. It looks like you put no thought into it and many shops are only taking contactless payments now.

Put a few squares of loo roll in the card instead. You'll be giving them something they could really use.

Smell My Cheese

Another week, another attempt to find a positive spin on the lockdown under which we are living.

New research has linked a loss of sense of smell with the

coronavirus. It could also be caused by another virus, so it's not a definitive test, but we can say that because of coronavirus more people will be unable to smell things for a while.

There are the obvious downsides to anosmia. We'll miss the scent of freshly cut grass or the enjoyable aroma of a meal being cooked. However, who's cutting their grass these days? Even if they are, you can't go out to enjoy it.

As for food, you're only missing the smell of more tinned goods being opened and plopped into a saucepan. The panic buying of a fortnight ago has left us with smaller food options now.

Before you get too sad, think of the benefits of losing your ability to smell. It means no one would mind being stood downwind of someone vaping. Normally they smell like they've sneezed into an Angel Delight but if we can't smell them, vapers will look like they're providing dry ice for a 1980s music video.

Public transport would be a treat without a sense of smell. If you find yourself crammed into the armpit of a fellow commuter you won't know if they have just had a shower or had a full day sat near the office radiator in a nylon shirt.

You'd never know which corner of the Overground platform was more frequently used as a toilet. Bliss.

It seems that in a modern, busy city a sense of smell may be holding us back and if we lose it we could find life easier.

It's just a shame that while coronavirus knocks out your nose you can't go outside to enjoy it.

Got My Goat

It is easy to focus on the negatives of the lockdown. That's because they are very apparent. Being tracked by police drones for going for a walk sounds like the kind of thing you'd get in a dystopian sci-fi film. It's also why I only leave the house if I am dressed like a postman.

I prefer to focus on the positives. Since us humans have been staying inside, the air feels clearer. I didn't notice at first because the only way I could see the air was through my windows and they haven't been cleaned since before the pandemic. The foot-and-mouth one.

When I took my Government mandated exercise I realised the air looks cleaner. I don't know if it smells cleaner, all I can smell is mask. Satellite images have shown that across the globe, cities have less pollution above them where people have been forced to stay inside.

Planes are grounded and cars aren't being used. I can hardly remember what it feels like to be impatiently beeped as you attempt the Magic Roundabout.

I'm not the only one preferring it with fewer people out and about. Have you seen the footage from Wales where mountain goats have come down into the town and have been running around the place? If they plan on doing this more often they may have to drop the mountain part of their name.

Isn't it shocking that this is how long it takes Mother Nature to replace humans? If we were suddenly gone from the planet it's only two weeks before some other species steps up.

By the time we come out of this we may find our role as the dominant species has been taken. I never thought it would be the goats who replaced us, I presumed it would be seagulls because they looked like they were ready and waiting, but I was wrong.

If we are locked down for three more months, by the time we emerge there may be goat societies to deal with. They'll run the councils. They'll have jobs. They will have great thinkers; they already have the beards so they can sit around stroking them.

They won't have the technology that we developed but they could create a basic subsistence living structure. They'd be good at farming because some of them will have seen how we do it.

At some point we humans will be in charge again. If we can't overthrow them, because goats are pretty strong, we simply have to wait till the goats have a pandemic. Goats famously eat pretty much anything, and that's what caused our coronavirus problem in the first place.

5G or not 5G?

How are you keeping entertained during the lockdown? I'm hoping you have just shouted, "By reading some excellent newspaper columns, Steve" but I won't hold my breath, unless I'm in a shop and someone walks within two metres of me.

I've been enjoying the new conspiracy theories. I love a good conspiracy at the best of times. One of my favourites is the Flat Earth theory that tells us there's no such place as Australia, which would mean the TV show Neighbours was part of an elaborate misinformation plot.

I normally enjoy reading some of the things the anti-vaxxers say but they have been oddly quiet since Covid-19 cropped up.

There are many conspiracy theories about coronavirus though. One says it was created in a laboratory in China. Why would someone do that? Are we guessing it was meant as a form of biological warfare? If so, it's not very good. If you created a weapon that has a fatality rate of two percent your boss would be furious.

Maybe he'd give you a second chance and ask, "The two

percent it targets, is it the strongest and youngest who would be hardest to fight in a war?" And then you'd be fired.

Another theory is that it's caused by 5G radiation from mobile telephone masts. Why would a mobile network want to create something that means we all stay in doors? I haven't used my landline this much since the 90s.

Why can't people listen to the science without trying to find some false take on things that doesn't make sense? A professor of virology surely knows more about this than some mate on WhatsApp yet these conspiracy theories are faster than the virus when it comes to spreading around the globe.

Or spreading flatly over the disc, if you're a flat Earther.

Sunbathers

Who would have thought the British weather would be problematically good?

Normally we work all week, the weekend arrives and the weather mocks us by chucking it down like a Noah prequel.

While we're all meant to be staying in the sun has been taking the chance to shine and really rub it in.

The Easter Weekend was always going to be a hard time to keep people inside. We know there are eggs hidden out there by the Easter Bunny somewhere but we can't go to find them.

Government messages told us to stay in but what could they really say? Normally if someone wants to appeal to your better nature they'd say, "What would Jesus do?" This is Easter we're talking about, so the answer to that question would be, "Go away till Monday," which isn't the kind of message we should be giving.

It's the sunbathers I have a problem with. Even if we

weren't under a lockdown I would rant about people sunbathing in public spaces. I don't want to see pasty white bodies strewn everywhere. At first glance it looks like Casper's friends and family have been massacred.

Going without sunbathing for the sake of everyone else's health isn't that much of a sacrifice. I don't know why people care about being bronzed, no one's going to see it, we're in a lockdown. If you want to lie down and sweat for hours just leave the heating on.

I thought that 2020 would be the year people said to themselves, "I won't irradiate the elastin in my skin this summer. I'll slow down my race towards looking like a handbag in lost property while I have the chance." But no, some people went out there and baked.

At least they were easy to recognise. The people who rushed out to break the rules and catch some rays had telltale sunburnt shoulders. I was tempted to give them a little slap on the arm as I said hello but, at two metres away, I kept missing.

If the actions of the selfish tanned people mean we see our right to daily exercise get taken away I will be furious. I haven't been going out exercising daily, I have stayed in eating my way into the record books, but it has felt like my choice.

If I can't go out for a run even if I wanted to, it won't feel like I'm being a rebel any more. They're ruining this lockdown for me.

Strictly Cursed

I know the current situation is hard for a lot of us. I am still trying to use this column to bring you the more positive angles on our lives in a bid to help morale.

I had thought that the lockdown would cause a reduction

in the number of extramarital affairs. I'm no doctor but if you can't get within two metres of someone it's a lot harder to break your wedding vows with them.

I am, yet again, probably wrong. It's becoming a worrying trend.

The TV show Strictly Come Dancing has come up with a plan to go ahead despite the lockdown. We did the same on The Mash Report. We film from our own homes. It's strange to perform the show without a live audience but I couldn't fit 400 people in my flat, so it's for the best.

It means I don't know what happens in the rest of the show until I watch it being broadcast on a Friday night. This week, after the main show at 10pm, BBC Two scheduled a repeat of an episode from last year. How cruel of them to make it so easy to work out how much weight I have gained in lockdown.

Strictly Come Dancing will go ahead without a live audience too, but they can't film in their homes. The rumour is they plan to isolate the professional dancers with their celebrity partners for months.

It's like they're trying to make them have affairs. This is a TV show that has probably ended more relationships than The Jeremy Kyle Show ever did. It was famous for the Strictly Curse when the couples only saw each other at work.

When you think about it, a TV show where the vain people who go on TV – and yes, I realise that includes me – are put with stunningly fit dancers and given the task of writhing around together for weeks, it's not a shock that some of them develop lustful feelings for each other.

It is a shock that the producers think the best move is to stop the celebs seeing their spouses while they're doing it. There'll be more nookie than you get in a series of Love Island.

Will this ruin our viewing pleasure? Probably not. I tune in for the gossip as much as the dancing. I'm sure it will still be a great series of Strictly. It's next year I worry about. All the dancers will be off on maternity leave.

Morale

As the weeks of lockdown go on trying to find the positive, morale-boosting angles of the news is definitely getting harder.

It is a very sad situation. Every day hundreds of families start the grieving process because of this virus. I know what they are going through. Just before the lockdown, my Mother passed away. I know what it is like to be struggling with bereavement while you're also struggling with living indoors.

While the cases of infection can increase exponentially, the positive news stories increase, at best, in a linear fashion. That is why I believe that, more than ever, it is important to find the things that can make us feel lighter.

Have you seen how clear the air is? It feels like I can see for miles because of the lack of cars and planes pumping out mess into the air. If I could get high up enough I'm sure I could see all the way to Europe, which would cheer the Flat Earthers up.

It feels like we now have greater respect for people who train, study, work hard and dedicate themselves to saving lives. Whether it's NHS workers or people working in care, we have learned how important they are.

Do you remember the banking crisis in 2008? They were bailed out because they were so essential but I don't remember standing at my window clapping for five minutes because someone bravely turned up to an office and still took their bonus at the end of the year.

What about Captain Tom Moore? He's the hero who, at the age of 99, walked around his back garden to raise money for charity. Thanks to that guy putting in more effort than most of us will ever do, there is £25million helping NHS charities. It was also good to read that the police didn't turn up to tell him he can't use his garden for sponsored walking.

While the families members lost are a large source of pain, I have seen the kind of heart-warming and supportive comments people have been posting on social media. I received some lovely comments myself, which really did help at a difficult time.

Facebook posts, tweets and comments online had become a place for nasty, snide massages. Before coronavirus people would use the Internet to be rude to people they'd never be rude to in person. If our time dealing with coronavirus brings out the better side of us, I'm feeling more positive already.

Idris Ideas

I've heard people speak about the "new normal". When the lockdown ends and things go back to normal it won't be the same normal that we were living before April.

Maybe we will be more grateful when we spend time with friends. Probably not. You know what we're like, we'll go back to gossiping in no time.

Maybe we'll appreciate the key workers more. Or maybe we'll take them for granted again.

One thing I am very sure we won't do in the post-Covid world is follow the advice of Idris Elba. The actor suggested we should put ourselves in quarantine for one week every year to remember this time.

As an actor, he is amazing. As a celebrity, he is great. As a planner of commemorations I think he should do more acting. Should we really ruin our economy on an annual basis just so we don't forget the virus?

We didn't do this for other illnesses. After Bird Flu we didn't have an annual Sneeze Into Your Elbow Week. After foot and mouth we didn't have a barbecue on its anniversary.

We also don't remember other life-changing national events in that way. After World War II ended people weren't turning off all the lights so we didn't forget The Blitz. Although by the time the 1970s came around there were power cuts, so it was close.

Idris also said of his self-quarantining plan, "Other species use it. It's called hibernation."

I'm not sure that's why animals hibernate. Are squirrels remembering the nut allergy outbreak of 1752? They also don't hibernate for a week, but I'm splitting hairs.

Life will be different. Scientists are also saying, if the vaccines don't work, we may face a smaller outbreak every winter flu season.

So Idris may get what he wants after all.

The 26

Sadly because of the lockdown and social distancing rules, this year I couldn't do the London Marathon.

It's OK, I understand that saving lives is more important than completing a race. As Spock would say, "The needs of the many outweigh the needs of the few," so I totally understand.

I also hadn't signed up for it, done any training or even taken up running, but it's nice that I can blame this on Covid-19 for a change.

I wasn't the only one prevented from competing on Sunday but it became another heart-warming lockdown story as people took up the 2.6 Challenge instead. In place of running for 26 miles people found other things they could do at home 2.6 or 26 times.

Many people did events in their gardens but I read about one athlete who was doing laps of his living room. It showed great ingenuity although probably bothered his other half if she was trying to watch something on TV.

Thankfully it wasn't all running as I'm not naturally gifted at sprinting or long-distance so I avoid those sports. If someone asked me to do a 1.6k I'd run a mile.

Swimming events happened too. A charity worker was in the news for swimming 2.6km in her back garden. Thankfully she had a paddling pool or it would have been even harder.

The award-winning mixologist, which is a fancy word for bartender, Paul Martin attempted to make 26 cocktails in 26 minutes. That's impressive. It was more impressive before the lockdown but some of us have been drinking so much we're getting near that hit rate without even trying.

There was Lynn Hedgecoe who walked around a six-acre field 26 times in 26 different outfits, including doctors' scrubs, a scuba suit and an Elvis costume. Firstly, maybe those scrubs should have been sent to a doctor. Let's not start the 2.6kg of PPE challenge.

She also could have called that a "Getting changed in a field 26 times" challenge. I'm sure there are people online who'd pay for that.

It's great that we can tailor these challenges to our abilities. I may not be able to run 26 miles, but I could eat 2.6 packets of biscuits. Actually I might fail that as there is no way I'd be able to stop with 0.4 of a pack left. Looks like I'll have to do the 26 pack challenge.

The point is, yet again, with all this bad news about the

coronavirus crisis, we see stories about kindness, people pulling together and indefatigable spirit. And with that spreading, we'll beat this lockdown challenge.

Lockdown or Lock In

I spend a lot of time thinking about the things I miss from before the lockdown. Most of all I miss being able to visit my father. He's in a care home and seeing all the news about the situation in the care sector terrifies me.

I also miss smaller things. I miss going to work. I miss driving. I miss showering on a regular basis. I also miss going to the pub.

Thankfully experts have been trying to devise a way that pubs could open while adhering to social distancing guidelines. The basic rules would probably include staying two metres away from everyone else in the pub. The problem zone will be the bar. Normally people crush together and desperately try to get served before it's their turn.

The post-Covid world might finally see an end to this terrible system. My suggestion would be to take the red rope from the VIP section (let's be honest, the Ps in those sections aren't really that I) and use it to create a bar queuing system similar to the ones you find in a Post Office.

We could even have a loudspeaker system that says, "Bartender number 5 please," when it's your turn.

One of the rules the experts have suggested is to limit each drinker to three drinks. This is the same as our air quality improving. Somehow this hideous virus is forcing us to live a better way.

The reason for the three-pint limit is to free up space for more drinkers once you have finished. I thought it was going to be to stop us getting drunk. That's when you make your bad decisions to get closer to people that you normally wouldn't want to go near. Alcohol changes who you fancy. It's the same cognitive effect that makes you find sweaty kebabs attractive.

We won't have to worry about people getting drunk. We'll all be wearing face masks, so three pints in all you'll have is a wet chest and a thirst.

They also say that cinemas and theatres could re-open but with half-empty auditoriums. They'd have to show the new version of Cats just to make sure.

Actually, showing that film might mean the cinema has no one in it at all but we could make it half-full by asking furloughed workers to attend. I know it's a sacrifice but it's either that or pick fruit for eight hours.

All of the rules will seem annoying at some point but I'd stick to all of them if I could get to visit my Dad again.

5 MAY

Tracking App

Imagine this headline before we'd ever heard of Covid-19: "The Government is asking you to put an app on your phone to track your every movement."

We'd be out on the streets protesting. We're not doing that now, mainly because we're not allowed on the streets in groups of more than two people. A protest march of two people just looks like someone getting a banner delivered.

Not that long ago we feared the invasion of our privacy that technology could bring. We've all heard the stories of people who were having a conversation near their phone about a holiday they wanted to go on and the next time they used their device there were adverts about holidays.

We feared we're being listened to by our phones. Back when I used to present the breakfast show on GWR I would have welcomed that extra listener.

We could soon be willingly adding an app to our phones to track where we have been and who we have been near. It seems a far cry from a few months ago when we were worried about the police using facial recognition. We don't worry about that now. That's because we'll all be wearing masks, so that facial recognition money was wasted.

If you are found to be infected with coronavirus the app will message everyone you have been near to tell them. Those people know to get tested and, if they have caught it, their app will message everyone they have been near. It's basically the system that works with STIs but a lot less fun during the transmission phase.

Some people think that being tracked like this will infringe our liberties, but the option on the table isn't app or no app, it's app or stay in lockdown. What infringes your liberty more, your phone remembering who you have been near or being forced to stay in your home?

Who gets access to the data is a concern. Some don't want the Government or businesses knowing where they have been. Others probably worry their other half will see it and they'll be looking for an incognito browsing mode. Even if the data won't be used intentionally, it could be hacked.

Normally this is the part of the column where I steer us towards my point of view but in this case I don't know. I am not sure where I sit on the safety versus freedom debate.

Don't worry, I'm sure the algorithms at Facebook and Google know what I really think about this though. I'll have a look online.

What's In A Name

Lockdown has taught me a lot about the effects of poverty. It's worrying to see your career disappear, I'll miss it, but I realise I was lucky before. Real poverty costs lives. The Office for National Statistics found that if you are better off you stand more of a chance of surviving coronavirus.

The ONS also found that if you are a man you have a

worse time with the virus. If you combine those statistics it shows that women must be earning more than men now. That'll cheer some people up.

The news has also shown that money affects the names you give to your children. Prime Minister Boris Johnson and Carrie Symonds welcomed their little bundle of joy into the world by naming him Wilfred.

He'll be known as Willy Johnson, both words with a shared slang meaning. I'd be worried about my child being picked on at school with a name like that.

My working class education taught me that you have to have a solid bully-proof name. If your name rhymes with something rude, you're done for. If it sounds silly, you'll be taunted by those sounds for years.

My surname is fairly safe but even I was called Fallon because it sounded a bit like a character in Dynasty.

I can't name a son Alan or a daughter Ellen. Nella would be nice but a palindromic name is a ticket to years of hell.

Posh people don't have that worry. Boris knows he is rich and influential so giving his child a name that's up there with Richard Member is fine. No one will dare to pick on little Willy.

Extreme wealth makes this effect worse. Billionaire Elon Musk has named his new baby "X Æ A-12". I'm being serious. He's had a child with the singer Grimes and they have given their baby a name that looks like Teletext when you have bad reception.

If I named a child X Æ A-12 Allen it would be bullied every day. It would be known as Typo for short. The big boys at school would give it a wedgie as they shout, "Is that a name or a Battleships move?"

In theory X Æ A-12 Musk should be bullied more because that surname makes it sound like a sex pheromone you can buy online. A billionaire as a dad makes all of that go away.

Strange names are the domain of the rich, successful and powerful. And thanks to the lockdown I've ended up with a career that fits being called Steve.

Alert

I have learned a lot in this lockdown. I have learned that the older the bananas, the better the banana bread. I have also learned that the same isn't true for meatloaf.

The bigger lesson has been about how many people don't obey rules. I went for my run the other day and saw loads of people out running too, but they were doing it differently. They were horizontal, motionless, lying down in the park and covered in sun cream.

I find it shocking that some people rank their ability to go sunbathing as higher than other people's safety. So it will be interesting to see how many people break the rule now it has changed from "stay home" to "stay alert".

I know that we can't ignore the economy. A failing economy will cost lives, but we also need people to be alive to have an economy. Good luck running your small business if all your customers have expired.

I know that I am biased on this issue. My father is in a care home and if I sit for a second and think about all the ways someone could catch Covid-19 and take it into that home, I start to panic.

Will changing from "stay at home" to "stay alert" make more people stick to the rules? What does it mean to be alert? Will I be tweeting tomorrow, "@mrstevenallen · Been awake for three days straight. Still no sign of virus but MUST STAY ALERT"?

When I think of being alert I think of Inspector Clouseau arriving home to find Cato hiding somewhere.

Being alert is great. I'm all for it. It'll mean fewer muggings and not as many people tripping on pavements but I'd really like it if we didn't have a second wave of an infection that could rob us of our loved ones.

A second wave is possible. Even in Singapore, which had been credited with a great coronavirus response, they had a second wave linked to some nightclubs. I remember my nights down the Lava Lounge back in the day and I can see how nightclubs could be a contagion risk. Or maybe it was that kebab I had on the way home.

Interestingly, a recent survey has found that 90 percent of us don't want the lockdown to be eased. In that case, why are we worried about the wording of some Government slogan? You don't need the Government to tell you what to do. If you want to stay home, do it. The more of us who stay home the better the odds your loved ones, and my dad, get through this.

Face Masks

The latest series of The Mash Report has now ended. It was fun to film a TV show in my front room. If I thought being on TV would mean I get recognised in the street I didn't count for Covid-19. I'm not in the street thanks to the lockdown and if I do pop out I'm not recognised, mainly because no one cares who I am, but I can convince myself it's because of the face mask.

Yes, I have given in to the pressure and bought a face mask.

I don't know why I was so reticent. I was worried about how I'd look. I know what you're thinking, "Steve, it's OK to have pride in your appearance but the more of your face you cover the more attractive you become." Thank you.

Wearing a mask is strange to us, so it was always going to

take a while to get used to. In the past it was mainly highwaymen and bandits who had them. Those are two groups that most of us don't want to belong to.

Now we're all wearing masks I feel a little sorry for the bank robbers. In the old days if you walked into a bank in a mask people knew what you were there for. Now that we're all masked-up they must have to queue for ages to get to the cashier they want to rob.

I don't feel too sorry for them though, if they're robbing a bank they're breaking lockdown rules.

The first problem I found with this new way of dressing is that the masks are all sold as "one size fits all". I can tell you not all heads are one size. I've tried on hats that boast the same and look like a baby being born.

The mask covers my nose and mouth but the elastic brings my ears out to the side like a Martin Clunes tribute act. That's OK though. If anything, it improves my hearing, which is important when you're trying to stay alert.

The other problem is that the face mask makes burping less fun.

I have opted for a black mask as it's slimming. I also thought it would look good on stage when I go back to performing at live comedy gigs. I might change my act because being a ventriloquist will get easier.

But I am happy helping to keep people safe. It gives me pride. You should see the look on my face.

Good Sense

I never thought I was going to be in favour of anti-lockdown mass gatherings. I thought this was a time to err on the side of caution and potentially save lives.

Then I read that the promoted mass gatherings at Coate Water and Lawns Park didn't take place, because no one turned up.

Well done, protesters, you stayed at home. That's the spirit.

You could have argued that protesting is work that you can't do from home. Protesters tend to wear masks anyway, so they would have been sticking to the rules they hate so much without even trying. It's reassuring that even anti-lockdown people are staying at home.

Meanwhile Boris Johnson has said he understands that people are finding the complex nature of easing the lockdown frustrating. It doesn't make much sense that you can have a cleaner come to your home, and therefore your parents could have a cleaner, but you can't go and visit your parents.

You could visit your parents if you went round to do all their cleaning. Many people reading that will think, "Oh well. I'm going to miss seeing the folks for the next few weeks."

Boris said he was going to rely on the, "Good sense of the British people". While I always enjoy a bit of flattery I'm not sure good sense is as prevalent as we'd hoped.

We live in a country where people need to have, "May contain nuts," printed on the back of the jars of peanut butter. What do they mean, "May"? That jar better contain nuts, or I've just bought some butter.

Some irons are sold with labels saying, "Do not iron clothes while wearing." We can't have abundant good sense and a need for that warning label.

During the coronavirus crisis there have been some epic displays of good sense deficits. There was a picture of someone on a train who had made their own mask. So far, so healthy. The problem was they had made the mask from a supermarket bag-for-life. It's not going to be a long life if you go round putting your head in plastic bags.

Should we put the safety of our vulnerable and elderly in the hands of people with so much good sense they torch a 5G mast? And then they are probably upset that they can't post about it on Facebook because they have suddenly lost their mobile signal.

I hope the number of people with good sense outweighs those without it. There are some hopeful signs. How many people showed good sense and didn't go to an anti-lockdown protest? Everyone. So well done us.

Sports Should Return

We need our sports back. I have memories from two years ago of watching the World Cup, sipping on a crisp lager and enjoying a pub beer garden. It feels alien now.

They have tried to bring sports back in other countries. In South Korea they used posters of crowd members to fill the empty seats. We could do that here in our football stadiums. OK, the crowd would sit there motionless, showing no excitement or ability to celebrate, but Leyton Orient fans are used to that.

I'm kidding. I'll say the same thing about West Ham fans later to keep it fair.

In Germany they have taken the idea a step further. You can pay to have a cardboard cut-out of yourself sat in a seat watching the game. Whichever company is offering this service, they are wasted on football games.

There are times when I've been invited to my other half's friends' weddings that I didn't want to go to. I'd pay good money to send a cardboard Steve there instead.

Sending a big photo of yourself is also lockdown compliant. When everyone else is dialling into that meeting via Zoom but you send a full-sized replica of yourself, you'll get noticed. Hello promotion.

Our cardboard cut-outs could actually have a better time than we are. They could sit in beer gardens. They could be in restaurants or be nearer than two metres to someone without fear of infection. I don't like the idea that copies would have a better life than the original humans.

But even if they could go to a pub and watch the footy on the TV, they wouldn't smile or look like they're enjoying it. Especially if they were watching West Ham.

I told you I'd do it.

Testing, Testing

Ever since the start of the coronavirus epidemic people have been shouting that the solution is to, "Test, test, test."

Now it looks like two of those suggestions have been listened to. The Government has said it will provide antibody tests on the NHS to check if a person has had coronavirus.

This is good news because Covid-19 can be asymptomatic. Even if you've had no symptoms over the last two months you may still have been affected.

Care staff will be prioritised, so if you want to be tested just get yourself a job in a hospital.

If that seems a little involved you can buy an antibody test. There are online retailers selling the kits, but it was Superdrug that trended on social media when people were upset that they were charging £69 per test.

The test itself apparently costs pennies to produce, so there is a large mark-up, but this is how shops like that work. I'm sure it doesn't cost much to make mint shower gel but they charge several pounds for it. The Original Source one boasts that it contains 7,927 mint leaves. Round it up and put 8,000 in, you tightwads.

It is a bit steep. When I heard they were asking nearly £70 for each test I thought, "What do they want, blood?!"

Then I read more about how the tests work and realised they do.

Many people were upset that they might have to pay for a test but it is important to remember, you don't have to get tested. They only tell you if you were ill with coronavirus in the past. The fact that you're not currently on a ventilator should tell you even if you've had it, it wasn't that bad.

At the moment the scientists aren't sure that having the antibodies means you'll be immune to the virus. It makes you wonder what the point of making antibodies is if they don't keep you well. Adding pointless cells into my blood is just making me weigh slightly more and I do not need help in that regard.

If you pay £69 for this test and you find out that you had the virus you could still be at risk, so you still have to stay at home. The only thing you can do with the information is bring it up at dinner parties, which we can't have at the moment.

But in the name of research, I will get myself tested. I need to pop to the shops for toothpaste and fake nails anyway. I'll let you know the results when I get them.

The Visit

It's a sentence that most of us never want to write but I have something in common with the Conservatives' political advisor Dominic Cummings. And I don't just mean the similar hairstyles we sport.

I took a long journey in the car to visit my father. The big differences in our situations are that I wasn't involved in telling everyone else to stay at home, I had no symptoms and I did it just last week when we were allowed to travel.

The reason for my journey was a birthday. That is or isn't a similarity between me and Dominic depending on who you believe.

My dad is 81. He lives in a care home because he has vascular dementia. I used to visit him all the time. One of the benefits of working as a stand-up comedian is that you tour the country so I was often near to where he is.

When lockdown happened I stayed at home. There will have been many people in that same situation. You want to visit your loved ones but at the same time you don't want to visit them. You don't know if you're carrying coronavirus and the guilt you would feel if you knew you passed it on would be huge.

When the restrictions were slightly eased I started planning with the care home. We arranged that I could stand outside the window in his room and wave happy birthday to him. It works. It's like window shopping but you know one of the mannequins.

On the day of the trip it was strange to be in a car. Thankfully I hadn't forgotten how to drive; it's like riding a bike, but way less liked by the cycling community.

I also regret parking under a tree just before the lockdown came in. My car looked like modern art, a metaphor for how we feel treated.

A three-hour drive each way was common when I was performing at live gigs but it felt longer this time. One reason is that public toilets are shut, so being at least six hours away from my home convenience brought out my inner camel.

The last time I saw my dad was the week before the lockdown kicked in. It was at my mother's funeral. I hadn't been able to visit and offer comfort for two months and sadly he can't understand why I'd stopped visiting.

I don't care much about who resigns or who keeps their jobs. I don't care much about which minister is wheeled out to explain or excuse. I just want the people in charge to have some respect for what we're all going through.

Check Myself

Typing this is harder than usual. Not in an emotional way. This isn't going to be a column about my ill father again. It is harder to type because I have just stabbed myself in the finger.

I've taken a coronavirus antibody test. For £70 you can see if you have already had the illness. I wasn't sure if it was a good idea. A few months ago I could afford to splash £70 on random purchases but since the lockdown has put my stand-up comedy career on hold I have been making my living by performing live video shows on YouTube every Tuesday and Thursday evening at 9pm. It'll take approximately most of 2020 to earn that £70 back but, seeing as I am saving money on haircuts and soap, I thought I'd risk it.

Doing the test feels like you're about to perform surgery only you don't have to wear a mask, which is one of the few things you can do these days without wearing one. I did mine in the kitchen. There's a risk that you will spill blood everywhere, and I eat my steaks rare so my kitchen is used to it.

You have to get the blood pumping before you start. They recommend doing a little exercise and then washing your hands in hot water. Alright, Mum! I get the hint.

Filling the tube with your own blood takes a while. As a proud Midlander there's a chance that mine is thickened with gravy, but the body doesn't want to give it up. You end up squeezing your finger like you're trying to get the last bit of toothpaste out.

After a while you get used to it and the blood flows easily. Seeing as I was in the kitchen I was tempted to squeeze out a little more blood and have a go at home-made black pudding. It would beat the recent trend of making sourdough bread.

I posted the sample and now I nervously wait to be contacted. It's a similar feeling to when you've been flashed by a speed camera and you check the post to see if you got a fine.

Regardless of the result I will have to keep to the Government guidelines of stay in, stay alert and only go to Barnard Castle if you have to. I'm taking the test purely out of curiosity.

If it comes back negative it will show I have successfully socially distanced but if it comes back positive it will make me feel lucky that I had a mild case.

I'll let you know the result. Fingers crossed. Ouch.

Space... A New Frontier

After weeks of feeling down about the coronavirus pandemic and the lockdown, I saw something on TV that has raised my spirits.

I had always been jealous of those who got to watch the moon landing in 1969 live on television. I had a very good excuse for missing it, I was many years away from being born, but I would have loved to have watched that moment in history.

We now have a modern version. I'll never forget where I was when I saw the SpaceX launch. I was at home. Of course I was, there's a lockdown on.

This modern spacefaring event was broadcast via the Internet in high definition, which shows how technology has advanced since the 1960s. Famously, Apollo 11 had less computing power than the modern day wristwatch, although to be fair, watches have far less rocket fuel, which may be more important. Sometimes brute force is more useful it seems, but that's not the lesson that cheered me up.

The new rocket can fly itself. I heard the commentator during the launch say that it can get itself from Earth, and dock with the International Space Station, on its own. The Falcon 9 rocket that gets the module into space can also fly back down to Earth and land itself on a drone ship.

Humans are hardly needed. I'm sure the hipsters of the future will offer artisan hand-steered space flights but in general the computers will be in charge. That didn't raise my spirits.

It must have been a strange feeling for the astronauts Bob and Doug because we are so used to being the ones in charge. They were sat there, feeling nervous but not being in control. I've had Uber rides like that.

It was also a space event of our time because it's about the money. When Nasa sent people into space it was to show what humanity could achieve. SpaceX sending people into space is the first time the private sector has done it. It's one small step for a company, one giant leap for tourism.

It won't be long before you can pay a huge amount of money to take your holiday in space. Yes, you will have to wear the spacesuit, the helmet and be trapped in a small capsule, but with the coronavirus quarantine rules here on Earth, normal flights will be like that anyway.

The reason I feel better after watching the launch is that it showed me that we can still meet challenges. Be it Spanish Flu or the Apollo missions, we did it once, we can do it again.

6 JUNE

I'll Drink To That

I went to a pub!

It feels like such a momentous event that I may celebrate it by going to a pub again.

Obviously I hadn't been to a drinking establishment in months. I hadn't become a paragon of temperance, I'd still been supping beers from the supermarket, but I hadn't been to a pub and I missed it.

Don't worry, this wasn't some underground speak-easy like prohibition era America, it was a local that has started doing what a lot of pubs have, selling beers to takeaway.

It was strange to have a pint of lager in cheap disposable packaging, that's normally what the kebab comes in later. The process was Covid-compliant. There were masks and gloves in all the right places. One barman served from the pub door and the queue down the street was spaced out at two metres between people. I liked that because I knew when I'd get served. In a normal pub setting I have to stand by the bar while louder people and those with better cleavages than me get served first.

I bought two pints and some peanuts. I only got the peanuts for the salt because the pub loos were still shut and I needed to absorb as much of that liquid as possible.

And then came the surprise. I was asked for £10.

I'd forgotten that beer was getting on for £5 a pint. I'd been so used to supermarket prices I nearly spat my mouthful of beer out in shock, but I didn't want to waste the 30 pence worth I had in there.

As lockdown relaxes we'll have to get used to paying for the service and experience, not just the product. It won't be long after we're let out that we may have to stay in to save money.

Till then I don't think I'll go back to the take-out pubs. Instead I plan to recreate the pub experience at home. I'll buy my beer in the supermarkets and then, on Friday night, I'll stand and queue for my fridge for half an hour. When I get to the fridge door I'll turn myself away because I have the wrong footwear on and then come back. Eventually I'll get my drink, I'll get some crisps and sit on my sofa with the TV on but muted. That way I can have no idea what's happening on the TV but it can still distract me from having a conversation.

At the end of the night I can throw £50 away and text my ex. Perfect.

More Rules

As we get used to the new rules of the altered lockdown it can be a little hard to know exactly what you are or are not allowed to do.

A few weeks ago we were in the situation where you could meet up with one friend in Lawns Park as long as you were sitting two metres away. You could also sit two metres away from a group of strangers. It didn't make any sense that you could sit next to more strangers than friends. And if you got chatting to that group of strangers and started to get on well, at what point did you have to tell all-bar-one of them to go away?

They clarified the situation by bringing in the new rules. You can have six friends in your garden. I'm sure it could be six strangers in your garden too, if that's what you're into.

It was a good rule for helping us to become a society again. All I have is a window box and it's not two metres long, so it doesn't help my situation, but if you want strangers in your garden, and you have beers, hit me up.

The problems came when the Government brought in the rule about what you could do with your romantic partner if you didn't live together. The rules say you can't go into someone's house unless it is for reasons of work.

That means you can have a cleaner come round but you can't have your boyfriend or girlfriend come over. At this point you haven't been intimate with your lover for two months and the Government won't let you get it on.

They didn't specify if you could do it in the garden but that would probably upset the six strangers you have in there. If that's what you're planning don't invite me.

Call me Mr Loophole but surely you could have your partner visit you as long as they do all your cleaning. Try suggesting that.

Thankfully they updated the rule and suggested that you could have romantic relations with your partner as long as you both wore face masks. It's better than the paper bag she's suggested in the past but will anyone stick to this rule? Even if they don't, it's impossible to police. The Government can't send PCSOs round to check if you kept your face mask on all the way through. If they could somehow catch you, surely they can't fine you for it.

If they do, just tell them you did it to check your eyesight. That seems to be a valid excuse these days.

Zzzzzz

There are so many ways in which our lives have been badly affected by the spread of this coronavirus. There's a new one to add to that list, it could be making us snore more.

Oh, the cruelty, a virus that makes us snore more but also stops us being able to sleep in an Airbnb to get some escape.

I read an interview with an expert, Stephen Makinde, who claimed that being trapped indoors could make us snore more when we're asleep. My first response was to think this was nonsense but then I realised, maybe this could be something else to blame my snoring on, so I read further.

You see, I am a snoring sufferer. Well, I don't suffer as much as the other half. I don't hear it because I am asleep at the time. The snoring has stopped by the time I am woken by a sharp prod and the words, "You're snoring again," shouted at me like she's been possessed.

It's hard to deal with because it's not deliberate. I don't lie there pretending to be asleep and making those loud snoring sounds just to keep her awake. Although now I've thought of that, it's a great move which I'll remember for the future.

I have always believed that snoring evolved to scare off big animals. What may be annoying now would have been keeping us safe in our cave a few epochs ago. That argument never seems to calm down anyone I've been sharing a bed with. I can't think why.

Snoring isn't deliberate but it has felt like my fault. In the past experts have said it may be linked to obesity, so the more I snore the more it felt like I should diet and exercise.

But now I can blame it on the pandemic. Phew.

The theory is that the feeling of being trapped in our surroundings can manifest itself as a physical restriction with our breathing. Maybe it's the feeling of being physically restricted by clothes that used to fit too.

I read more of the interview with the sleep expert and he said that being forced to spend more time with your partner in an unhappy relationship might make your snoring worse.

What can be done? We can't get out of the house more, we can't feel better about the stressful time we're living in, but our partners can be nicer to us.

It's either that or sleep on our sides, but it's worth a try.

Retail Therapy

The shops are open again. I'd celebrate but I don't have any champagne in and I'm not going to the shops to get some. Have you seen the queues?

After months where the only shops open were the ones that sold essential items, we have finally got the non-essential shops back. Some stores reported queues of up to a mile. I would have been more impressed with them if the people in the queue weren't forced to keep two metres apart. Most of those queues were empty space. It's like hearing there's a seven mile queue on the M1 then realising most of it is made up of cars that don't move forwards when there's a gap.

Isn't it fascinating that people are more excited about buying things they don't need than the items they can't get by without? The food shops have seen a normal level of demand but as soon as you could buy more clothes at Primark we all went crazy for it. I'm not sure why because even if you get a nice new outfit it's not like you're going anywhere to wear it.

If there is one thing I have learned during lockdown, while I've been at home doing comedy shows over Skype, it's that tinned food is essential but clothing items for the lower half really are not.

If you follow the logic you'd think that the way to make loads of money is to sell things that people will never use. That's why I'm opening a shop selling things like fingerless latex gloves, distressed face masks and the most useless item of all, indicator bulbs for BMWs.

I had thought that weeks of only buying the things we need might have helped us break the shopping habit. I'm not saying you should only spend money on the bare essentials – if I did that I'd never sell any tickets to these streaming comedy shows I'm doing – but I'd hoped our priorities had changed. I thought we'd learn to value the joy of a walk in the park, being out in nature, rather than sifting through piles of clothes.

Maybe we have learned to value spending time with our loved ones, but you can have too much of a good thing. At least a mile long queue gets you out of the house for a while.

Hold my space, I'll be there just as soon as I've found where I left my trousers in April.

Everydaycation

First we called them holidays and that was nice. Then came the trend of calling them vacations, which came from America and I didn't like it because vacating something reminds me of public toilets.

Then came 'staycation', blending vacation and staying, which really should cancel each other out. It's used to describe going on holiday to somewhere in the UK, which we used to call "going on holiday" before this word came along to make us feel bad about not going abroad.

Now we have a new one. Thanks to the coronavirus pandemic lockdown, we can't go on holiday and that is now being called an 'everydaycation'.

The concept is that instead of going somewhere, which is against the lockdown rules unless you're Dominic Cummings, we should stay at home and treat it like it's a holiday.

It's easy to start. A lot of us don't have work, which is quite like being on holiday. I have been eating food that I wouldn't normally try. On holiday that would be local cuisine and in lockdown it's mainly tinned goods, but it's all part of the everydaycation.

I like the idea. We should be good at enjoying our lives just as much when we are trapped at home as when we are on our holiday. I've never understood why some people live their lives only enjoying two weeks out of the 52.

So join me in making the next few weeks of lockdown as good as a trip abroad. On the first day wake up as early as you would if you were going to an airport, which is ridiculously early. I can't be the only one who has a 1pm flight and somehow works out that means I need to get up at 3:50am just in case.

Feel like you're on the continent by putting your clocks forward one hour. To be fair, you did that already back in March, so you're ahead of the game.

We have been forced to use contactless payments so that even the British Pound Sterling feels like strange money and that adds to the holiday feel.

Do not take it too far. Do not drive on the wrong side of the road. It's dangerous. If you want to feel like you're in a foreign country simply speak English but loudly and slowly.

I think the point I am getting at is while we are prevented from doing the things we enjoy let's take the time to enjoy what we can do. Lockdown doesn't have to be worse than a holiday. And look on the bright side, you'll only lose your luggage if you try really hard.

The Great Reopening

The Prime Minister has said that "our national hibernation" is coming to an end. I don't feel like I have hibernated because most animals wake up in the Spring much thinner than before.

We are definitely in a new phase. While it doesn't mean we are out of the lockdown completely we should get stuck in and enjoy our new freedoms. You know me, I am always on hand to try to find the positive.

The pubs are going to reopen. You will have to register to go in, which is a good thing. I have seen people in my local Wetherspoon's drinking pints early on weekday mornings and they look like they will struggle to remember their name later in the day. It's good that it's written down somewhere.

There are guidelines telling pubs to stop people dancing and not to play loud music. Apparently loud music might make us shout to be heard and that increases the spittle we flob out.

While banning music and dancing sounds like a real life version of Footloose, it's actually turning the pubs into the kind of place I'd like. At my age I want a sit down and a chat with a pint. Admittedly, the people I'm with might prefer my words being drowned out.

Restaurants can open but if they can't have people two metres apart they have to be one metre apart plus some other form of protection, such as a face mask. I've never tried to eat while wearing something that covers my mouth but I imagine there'll be a lot of diners asking for their food to be popped in the blender, and a straw.

There are some oddities to the guidelines. Hairdressers can reopen but nail bars can't, and nails are definitely further away from your mouth and nose than your hair is, unless you have some issues. Nail bars could operate normally but hairdressers ask you where you've been on holiday this year. That won't work in 2020.

I suppose the difference is that we can trim our own nails but after months of the hairdressers being closed a lot of people look like the 1970s are back.

As a stand-up comedian, I am saddened that live comedy isn't allowed back but bingo is. I think it's because the ruling powers don't want us satirists back at work, holding them to account. The solution would be for the bingo callers to add in some satire. "Eyes down, first number. Number of U-turns this week… 9."

Whatever you get up to, do it safely, or we'll be back here again.

Echo Beach

When Boris Johnson announced plans for some of the rules to be relaxed I felt really positive that we were heading towards the end of this thoroughly annoying time. The Prime Minister said he would be relying on the good sense of the British people.

I'm British and I have good sense. I'm not one of those people who need a label that says "may contain nuts" on a bag of nuts, or the words "for external use only" on a tube of Savlon. I've never been so hungry that I've looked at Savlon and wondered how it would work as a dip for some nachos. I have good sense and you have good sense, as you are showing right now by reading this column. So what could go wrong?

The sun came out and everyone forgot about good sense

and headed to the beach. When I saw the pictures of people flocking on Bournemouth I have never been more pleased that Wiltshire is a landlocked county.

The rules are simple. You have to stay two metres away and if you can't do that you have to stay one metre away and take some other form of precaution, for example a face mask.

Why would you want to lie in the sun if you're wearing a face mask? Tan lines on your back are bad enough but no one wants a two-tone face. You'll look like a telephone from the 1970s.

If you turn up to a beach and there's not enough space to be two metres away from everyone else you should go home. I understand that's easy for me to say. You would have spent ages on the roads to get there, so it will be annoying. And I like my personal space more than most. I think it comes from being a tall person. If you're stood within one metre of me I am worried that you're going to pickpocket me.

I realise that, yet again, this is another week where I, a so-called comedian, at least that's what people call me on social media, am advocating having less fun. All we are being asked to do to fight a deadly disease is stay away from people for a while, so it's not much.

I also know people like to get a tan because they think they look better with one. Remember, most of us are working from home via Skype or Zoom these days. All you need to do is go into Settings on your computer, look for Devices, find your webcam and alter the hue. There you go; instant tan without risking lives. You're welcome.

7 JULY

P Day

It's nearly P Day. After months of being stuck at home, the day of the pub is nearly upon us. I am getting ready for my first pub visit. I have my contactless payment card, my hand gel and I have stopped washing; that should keep people at least two metres away.

We have been told to drink responsibly, which is always easier said than done. Drinking can be an act that makes you less responsible as you do it. I have never become more responsible as the night has gone on. I've never woken up the next morning to find that, in a drunken haze, I joined the local neighbourhood watch scheme.

We have to be careful or we might end up like Leicester, and no one wants that. It's the first place in the UK to be subject to a local lockdown. While we're enjoying a nice pint the people of Leicester will be trapped at home once more.

Local lockdowns are strange because they have an edge. There will be a place where one street is in lockdown but the next street along is free. We could see a situation where you could find it easier to travel back from Spain than nip round to your neighbours.

On that topic, I am not sure I believe what the Government says about removing quarantine from some countries. When I had my first job in a factory the old guys working there pulled the classic prank on me. They sent to me to the stores to get a glass hammer, a left-handed screwdriver and a bubble for a spirit level. I was young and foolish and I fell for it. I felt so silly afterwards. So when the Government starts talking about "air bridges" I'm not falling for that one.

The big worry is that people in a local lockdown will travel to other towns to go to pubs and restaurants. Keep an eye out. Nottinghamshire is one place the Leicester escapees might try to visit.

As we're enjoying a drink at the weekend, we should keep an eye out. You might see someone trying to do our accent. If they use "duck" in the wrong way or if they don't know that "sen" means "self", dob them in. If they don't know that going "om" is what you do at the end of the night and isn't anything to do with meditating, call the police.

That must be what they mean when they tell us to drink responsibly.

Super Saturday

It seems like Swindon can pat itself on the back after Super Saturday. We didn't fall into the trap of overdoing it, like so many other places in the country.

Some of the pictures from London show drinkers giving up on social distancing. They were packed into the streets up close to each other. It looked like the headline should be, "Government downgrades how far a metre is!"

Elsewhere there were pubs shut early because of fights.

It's evidence of our strange relationship with alcohol. We should have predicted it because of Dry January. Once a year, there's a campaign to abstain from booze during the most depressing month. I think the concept is if you can stop drinking during the month with the least daylight and the longest gap between paydays you can do anything.

On the first of Feb we always see pictures of revellers out on the street, fully tanked up, wearing McDonald's bags for shoes. We don't do that in any other month. Those who have done Veganuary don't end it with a massive Atkins diet binge and pictures in the newspaper of them with the meat sweats. After Stoptober, November doesn't start with people finishing off the huge pack of cigarettes they got in duty free.

We only act like this when alcohol is involved. Super Saturday also saw the hairdressers reopen, but we weren't met with scenes of hairy people filling the streets outside the barbers downing the liquid they keep the combs in.

Maybe the powers that be could see this coming. There is a conspiracy theory online that says the Government may have wanted us to go overboard with the celebrating. If there is a second wave it will seem like the fault lies with the drinkers and not with the authorities.

If that's the case, we can hold our heads high because we didn't see crazy scenes in the SN postcodes. We won't be going through what so many others will be. They'll be getting phone calls from the track and trace people telling them that someone in the massive crowd of drinkers they were in on Saturday night has tested positive for Coronavirus and they should now quarantine for 14 days.

I have had some large nights out in my time but I have never been out on a session that required me to take two weeks off work.

Over the next few weeks the people who like to overdo it

will be stuck at home self-isolating, like their own mini Leicester. That's when I'll pop out for a nice quiet drink. I'll see you there.

Dinner Time

Do you fancy going out for dinner? I'm not offering to pay, but the Chancellor is.

Rishi Sunak announced that we will be getting our restaurant or pub bills cut in half. He's becoming the Groupon chancellor.

I hope this doesn't mean that after we've used our Government voucher we'll then get emailed all the time about cut price deals on waxing treatments. To the best of my knowledge I have never been waxed and yet Groupon have me on a list of people who might be interested.

The Government deal is that if you dine out in August, from Monday to Wednesday, you will get 50 per cent off. It feels strange to know that a member of parliament is buying us dinner. I remember politics in the 1980s so it seems strange to be getting a meal from an MP without it being part of some sleazy tryst.

The scheme is called Eat Out to Help Out and of all the Government plans to save our economy this is one I can do well at.

When they announced plans to get furloughed Brits to pick fruit I knew my back would give out. When they spoke of plans to get young workers back into jobs I saw myself in the mirror and had to admit I'm old now. When they planned to pause stamp duty I knew I wasn't going to move house, I hate packing.

Eating, however, is something I am good at. If anything, during lockdown, I have improved my eating skills. I certainly put the hours of practice in.

When my grandchildren ask what I did during lockdown I can say, "I helped by ordering a starter when I didn't need one. And that's why I still get these waxing emails to this day."

Save Our Steves

What do I have in common with whales and the NHS? It's not that we're all larger than we probably need to be.

There have been campaigns to save us. Not me in particular, but the Save Live Comedy campaign has been launched and it's receiving a lot of support.

When the lockdown kicked in, the live comedy industry went away. For many of us who made our living by performing in clubs it was a blow. Months later and we still don't have our careers back.

Gyms are opening but comedy clubs stay closed. The experts say that laughing indoors could emit infected aerosols but have they seen how people grunt and pant in gyms? When I go to the gym I also hear a lot of laughter but that might be because of the shorts I'm wearing.

Indoor pools are opening. Surely you're more likely to catch something in a pool than a comedy club. We were never made to walk through a foot bath before entering a comedy gig.

It may have been our fault. As an art form, stand-up comedy has spent most of its time since the 1980s being sarcastic about politicians, so it's no surprise to find that the people in charge aren't in a rush to let us start again.

I also realise that we stand-up comedians are not an essential service. No one will be clapping for us like they did the NHS. Well, people will be clapping for us but I think that's out of convention. It's always amazed me that when you are a performer you get a round of applause as you walk on the stage. That's before the audience could know if you're rubbish or not.

It's not simply an issue of being essential any more. Nail bars aren't essential. Hairdressers aren't essential when you have the amount of hair I have. Live stand-up comedy is something we do well. We have possibly the best circuit in the world. Through the years I have met many acts who moved to the UK because it's the greatest place to perform live.

In the UK, we pride ourselves on our sense of humour. If you love something you have to put some work in to keep it alive. Many people love a night out where you can relax, forget about the troubles of the world, have a good laugh and recharge the mental batteries before going back to real life.

I hope that before too long I get to see you at a live comedy gig. Trust me, it's better than seeing me down the gym.

Manly Masks

Men. We are great. I know the media keeps making us look bad, adverts portray us as idiots and it can feel awkward when we point out that we do some things well. However, right now, we're not helping our own cause.

Research has found that men are more likely to object to wearing a face covering because we feel they make us less manly.

Oh, come on, it's only a mask. It's not a ponytail, and to be fair some very manly roadies at music gigs have ponytails. They lug huge speakers around all day and you wouldn't want to mess with them.

Think about what you're risking. Even if wearing a mask makes you feel slightly less butch, I imagine lying in a hospital bed relying on a ventilator might make you feel worse.

I don't agree that all masculinity is toxic, so let's use it. If you want to feel manly you simply have to change how you feel about masks. Shredder from the Teenage Mutant Ninja Turtles cartoons, Jason from the Friday the 13th films and Iron Man all have face coverings and they are some of the manliest men around.

Even Hannibal Lecter kind of wore a mask and you wouldn't call him a little girl's blouse and get to keep your kidneys.

There are many things that, rightly or wrongly, feed into a man's sense of self. We like to feel useful, like we can provide and protect. Those services might not be needed – no one is saying only men can do those jobs – but as a man it is programmed into us to want to have that value. Wearing a mask helps us do that. It may keep us healthy so we can keep working. It may protect others around us if we have Covid and we don't know because we're so manly we don't feel any symptoms. We can protect our families by setting a good example by wearing a face covering.

Not all masks are manly. I watched The Masked Singer and it didn't bring out my manly side. All we need to do is pick a manly looking mask and we can solve this problem.

Imagine how tough you'd feel walking around in a mask like Bane from the Batman films. OK, you'd stop feeling tough and start feeling stupid as soon as you did the voice that goes with it, and we all know you'd do the voice.

If you want the manliest thing of all, I could send you a mask with a print of my lockdown beard on it. Embrace the manliness.

Good News (for Jeff)

Are you tired of reading about how bad the economy is going to get? Sick of hearing about V-shaped recessions, U-shaped recessions or even a W-shaped one if there's a second wave of infection? Maybe this will cheer you up.

There is news about someone doing well out of this pandemic. It's Jeff Bezos. He's the man behind the Amazon website and he's the richest man in the world.

It's actually an impressive achievement to be the richest man in the world when you remember that he has been through a divorce. He could easily have ended up with the title of "ex-husband to the richest woman in the world".

In the space of one day recently Jeff got over £10billion richer. That should keep him going for a while. He's a long way off not knowing where the next meal is coming from. I'm sure he has Amazon Prime, so he could get one delivered within a day.

The reason Jeff is richer is thanks to us. During the pandemic we have been staying away from shops and buying things online. I can understand why. If you shop online you don't have to stand in a queue and you don't have to wear a mask. Heck, you don't even have to wear trousers.

Many experts have been saying that this way of shopping will hit our economy. People have talked about the benefits of working from home for years. It saves on travel so it's better for the environment. You don't have to wear anything on the lower half so it's better for naturists. You don't buy things from shops on your way into work so it's better for you bank balance.

Now it seems that having to pop into a shop for a lunch that you don't really fancy at a price you don't want to pay was the only thing keeping our economy going.

The money that has gone from our economy must have

gone somewhere. And now we know it all went to Jeff Bezos.

Mr Bezos is now estimated to be worth £148billion, which means his worth is only £11billion less than the GDP of Greece. To be fair, Greece isn't that well off. Have you seen their tourist attractions? They're in ruins. They should think about getting some new ones. They're richer than Jeff Bezos, for crying out loud.

I'm sure the news that Jeff Bezos is now even richer will make us all feel happier as we worry about our jobs. What a world.

Fat Chance

I am fat. I know this because I calculated my body mass index. I then tried to work out ways that I could prove BMI to be an unreliable measure. The classic case to mention is rugby players. Their BMIs are often in the overweight range but they're athletes.

I, however, am not an athlete. And if the only sportspeople I can compare myself to are the ones known for downing pints, it's a pretty weak argument. Deep down I know it's right.

It's something we might be hearing more. Part of the Government's new plan to get us fitter is to tell GPs to be frank. Our doctors should tell us, "You're fat."

I know what I'm like, I am oversensitive and I don't take criticism well. When my doctor tells me I am fat I will probably retort with, "Well, playing golf isn't exactly keeping you in shape either!"

Some people make the case that fat shaming, as it is known, isn't going to help people. If something makes you feel bad you might turn to food to make you feel better.

I know what that's like. I "eat my feelings", as they say,

and my feelings taste great.

I am not sure that your doctor would be fat shaming you in this instance. I presume your GP will only tell you the news and doctor-patient confidentiality prevents them from shouting, "Give way for fatso," as you leave their office. They won't post it on social media.

The only person who will know that you've been called out on your unhealthy size is you, so you could tell everyone in your life that you got a clean bill of health.

If the doc ever tells me I'm too large I'll report back that he said I was in great shape for a rugby player.

So, while I don't agree that these actions are fat shaming, I am not convinced that it will help. As a large chap I can tell you that us fat people are fully aware that we are fat.

You may think you're bringing some new information to our attention but please remember, we see ourselves fresh out of the shower. We know what it's like when we bend down to tie a shoelace and feel our stomach push one of our lungs into our neck. We were there when we had to undo our belt after winning at an all-you-can-eat buffet lunch. They are a competition, right?

I don't know what the answer is, but I have a feeling this isn't the solution. And you can trust my feelings, they taste great.

8 AUGUST

New Rules Again

A new survey has found that only half of us understand the new lockdown rules.

If this survey was done by asking people to stop in the street and speak to a stranger with a clipboard, it's missing all the people who think we're still not allowed to leave the house, so the real figure could be much worse.

It was easy when the rules were simple. We were told to stay at home, so as long as you could remember where you lived you had it covered.

Now we find ourselves in a situation where it's hard to make sense of it all. You can meet your friends indoors as long as there are only two households meeting. You could meet up with several households if you did it in a pub, which is indoors. If your friends own a pub, how many households could visit?

We're lucky in Wiltshire that we have avoided any extra restrictions but if one of your friends lives in Greater Manchester or Leicester, they can't meet up with other households but they can still go to pubs as long as they only see people from their own household. If they visit a pub in Wiltshire they'll come across very aloof.

If one of your friends has recently come back from a part of Spain with a lower infection rate than the UK, they're less likely to have coronavirus than your other friends but they can't go anywhere as they're under quarantine for two weeks.

You can go to a beauty salon but you can't have anything done to your face. I thought the face was where most of us wanted to look beautiful. We could see a lot of "body for Baywatch, face for Crimewatch" situations. That's OK because most of us have no idea if we can go down the pub or not, so no one is going to see what you look like.

In England we're still meant to stay 2 metres apart if you're not wearing a face covering. In Scotland the 2 metre rule has been eased to 1 metre. So if you're stood by the border you have to be 2 metres away from your Scottish friend who only has to be a metre away from you.

If you go to a cafe you have to wear a face mask if you're taking the coffee away and therefore aren't spending that long in the shop, but if you're staying in and breathing more you can be barefaced.

All we want is clear advice from the Government. I'd drink to that. But I am not sure where.

Don't Make Us Pick

Many parents will be thinking, "Oh, what I wouldn't give to get these children back to school." Now we are faced with actually answering that question.

Prime Minister Boris Johnson has said that reopening schools is a "national priority", which means other things may have to close.

The first time we heard of this ultimatum was when Professor Graham Medley from the London School of Hygiene and Tropical Medicine spoke about it as an option. I always thought the name of that academic establishment really takes a leap half way through. "School of Hygiene," sounds like wiping work surfaces down. "And Tropical Medicine," is that Parrot fever?

So when Prof Medley mentioned it, I started to worry. Many people think that school children should be back to learning for the good of society, but don't make us pick between that and having a pint.

At first, I wasn't sure why we'd have to shut pubs to let schools open. Is there a shortage of bouncers that are needed for both? The UK brought in restrictions on opening hours for pubs during the First World War to stop workers in munitions factories drinking too much. Is that the problem with Year 7s now?

While opening schools would help parents cope, some of them may need the pub too. Don't make us choose.

Surely there are other types of shops that we could close up again to open the schools. Tattoo parlours are open. If we shut those we could still have pubs open. In fact there's an argument to be made that you shouldn't have pubs and tattoo parlours open at the same time anyway. It'll stop people having the name of the person they've been dating for a week put on their back.

Shutting shops to open pubs would be a better solution. A lot of shops are shutting on their own. If we tally up WH Smiths, Debenhams, Pizza Express and Victoria's Secret does it buy us a few classrooms?

I'd also nominate candle shops. Do we need so many? I haven't had a power cut in years. I dated someone a while back who bought many candles but never lit them. She said she bought them for the fragrance. If you can relate to that, try air fresheners. They'll blow your mind.

Card shops could go too. In an age of email we don't need to send cards, and during a pandemic we shouldn't sell anything you lick and put in the post.

I think we could close some shops before the pubs, but knowing my luck the Government will agree with me and then they'll pick the off licences.

Exam Time

It's that time of year again when we stop complaining that it's not hot enough and start complaining that it's too hot. Well also spare a thought for those getting their exam results.

It's always a worrying time. The closest I get to that nervous feeling of anticipation these days is when the car is in for its MOT.

This year has been even harder. Thanks to a certain virus, that has received more than enough publicity, pupils couldn't take their exams. What has gone in place of the exam system has been a mess.

Someone came up with an algorithm which, when you remember we haven't been given a track and trace app that works yet, was ambitious. We have spent years hearing that our phones are tracking us and storing data about us and then we find that the Government can't use these phones to track our data.

This algorithm highlights what is wrong with the class structure in the UK. It worked out that children from poorer backgrounds shouldn't be getting good grades. It's the computer version of a posh person saying, "This won't do at all. If poor children get the same results as middle class children then it's not fair to those parents who spent their hard-inherited money to get an advantage."

It's not the algorithm's fault. It simply worked out that the education system is biased in favour of the middle classes and tried to copy that.

If you have received some results, I hope you got what you wanted and weren't affected by the flaws in the system.

If it helps, I can tell you this. I am in my forties and I don't know anyone who's still bothered by their exam results. One day it'll be OK.

Back to Work

After months of being jobless I have finally returned to work. Being a stand-up comedian was a dream of mine from an early age. I like the anti-establishment, rebellious feel to the job. We often act like outlaws.

Then the lockdown happened, the Government made performing in clubs illegal and we were actually outlawed, which turned out to be less sexy than I had always imagined. It involved more sitting at home and watching Netflix than I'd hoped.

Finally my joblessness has ended. I have performed stand-up again. Over the weekend I performed at a drive-in comedy show. It's basically shouting at people in a car park, which I am pleased to say was a first for me.

When the audience were enjoying the jokes, instead of clapping, they beeped their horns. There was one part of my act where someone was beeping their horn all the time. If felt great. It wasn't till after I realised it was a car alarm going off.

It was the first time I had performed live in person since March. I had done a few online gigs, which taught me a lot. I had always thought I looked terrible on camera phones but I now realise that was because the only photos I saw of me were taken by my partner. She'd get her phone out, take two dozen pictures and then spend ages going through them deleting the ones she didn't like.

In the photos she kept she looks great but my face looks like I was smiling, sneezing and breaking wind all at once. She posts those things to social media. If you see her Facebook profile it looks like she's dating someone doing Goonies cosplay.

I think that's why, when a couple splits up, you'll see her friends posting on her wall, "He was punching above his weight, hun." Well, yeah, if you judge it by those pictures.

Online or drive-in gigs still lack the atmosphere of real stand-up comedy. The art form is at its best when it's done in an underground, cramped bar. Basically, what we stand-ups need to succeed are the same things that make coronavirus thrive.

I should have asked previous audiences to stop washing their hands before a show, I could have received better reviews.

It was nice to be earning again but I will admit I was rusty. It's been a while since I did any performing. You try taking a four month break and then trying to do your job in a car park.

So, as we go back to work, we should probably cut ourselves some slack.

Oh No It Isn't

The panto isn't happening this year. Oh, yes it is. Oh, no it isn't. It actually isn't.

I was sad to read that the Queen's Theatre in Hornchurch postponed this year's pantomime. If I am honest, I haven't been to see one in ages. The last time I was in a panto audience was when I'd started dating an actress who was starring in one. No one tells you how silly you'll feel as a fully grown man going to see a panto on his own.

The Government has allowed theatre performances to take place, but the COVID-compliant restrictions make many shows unsustainable. The audience has to be spaced out. That can affect ticket sales revenue.

For pantos, social distancing causes more problems. When the villain walks on stage the crowd will have to shout, "He's behind you. Hopefully two metres behind you!"

It is understandable that local shows can't go ahead when even big West End extravaganzas have struggled. Earlier this year the Phantom of the Opera run came to an early end because of the lockdown restrictions, which is a shame because the main character in that is already wearing a mask.

They could have followed in EastEnders' footsteps and made the pantos with safety protocols in place. Cinderella wouldn't have gone to the ball because she would have been in lockdown. Snow White would have been bubbling with the Seven Dwarfs but one was Sneezy, so that would trigger 14 days of quarantine.

Aladdin would have rubbed that lamp but would it still wake the genie if you're rubbing it with an antibacterial wipe?

Hopefully pantos will return in 2021, just in time for them to be cancelled because men play the old women and women play the boys and that'll offend someone, I'm sure.

Train Tickets

We are all being asked to get back to work. The powers that be want to get the economy up and running again and for that we have to pack our briefcases, find something to wear on the lower half and head into the office.

The middle step is quite difficult. I'd packed away anything I hadn't worn since winter, and that included all my trousers.

Given that they want us to commute it's surprising that they have announced a train fare increase of 1.6%.

It is because some ticket prices are linked to inflation and at 1.6% it's lower than we have had for a long while, but the reason inflation in low is because the economy took a hit. Who do they think will be able to afford to pay more?

They're expecting us to travel in and have less time with our families, all while wearing a mask and paying extra for the privilege. It sounds like 1.6% more of a reason to keep working from home to me.

Independent watchdog Transport Focus has said train companies should change the way the ticket system works to reflect the change in our working patterns. Does that mean they want train companies to sell us tickets to our own homes? They already do that, it's called a return.

As we go back to work it is likely we'll go in for two or three days a week but with a season ticket you're paying as if you'd go in every week day. An annual season ticket from Barking already costs £2,076.

It's a bad time for train tickets to price themselves out of our reach. At the very least it feels like the price hike should be delayed. If there's one thing train companies are good at, it's delaying things.

9 SEPTEMBER

Bye Left-Wing Comedy

It took a long while to get stand-up comedy happening again. Tattoo parlours, gyms and flights were all happening weeks before we could come back. I picked those examples because, like a stand-up comedy gig, they collectively include tightly packed crowds breathing out a lot, and regret.

It's not a surprise. If an industry spends decades mocking Governments it makes sense that the Government would drag its heels to let it start up again.

Has comedy mocked all Governments equally? That seems to be the issue at hand as we hear the new Director General of the BBC plans to tackle the perceived left-wing bias in comedy.

The Telegraph has reported that Tim Davie believes the BBC's comedy output is seen as too one-sided. I don't want to fall out with the new boss before he's even unzipped his pencil case.

As a comedian on BBC Two's The Mash Report I have

accurate memories of sitting behind the newsdesk reading out jokes about Jeremy Corbyn, patronising Remainers and hipsters. When you hear some ranting voice saying that you never hear a joke about the left, those memories prove to me it's not true.

So we can move onto the issue of balance. Do you see more jokes about the Tories than Labour? Yes. I had to work harder to remember the lampooning of the left than I would to recall all the times we've mocked the Tories. Is that a problem?

A satirical show will mock the government of the day more than the opposition because – and this may sting a little if you're in opposition – the Government's actions are more important. The Government makes decisions that impact lives. If there's a joke that can reveal an inherent flaw in the logic of that decision, it deserves to be done.

The opposition may come up with some plan that will never happen. That's like mocking DFS for ending their sale. You always have plans. Come back to me when it might actually happen.

Being in leadership requires pragmatism and compromise, which will create flaws and hypocrisies, which some of us will dash to point out. If you're not in charge you have the luxury of sticking to your ideology. It's less practical but leaves less space to muck up and receive a good ribbing.

From the point of view of comedic theory, who do you think will inspire more jokes, Boris Johnson or Keir Starmer?

Boris Johnson has spent years playing the fool and doing interviews saying how he likes to play the fool. He's in on the joke. We've all heard the stories of how he messes his hair up before he goes on stage. He's Milton Jones with an 80-seat majority.

If you add in the times he hid in a fridge, dangled from a zip wire and rugby-tackled a child, he is a gifted physical comedian in the style of Eric Sykes.

For most of the series of The Mash Report the left has been figure-headed by Jeremy Corbyn. Thank heavens he made his own jam, or there wouldn't have been much in there to detect as a person.

Not only do I remember doing jokes about Jeremy Corbyn, I also remember the response. I am new to TV so I would excitedly browse Twitter as the show was going out only to see loads of angry thumbs had sent messages saying, "Typical left wing comedy," "bunch of lefties" and then, "Typical Corbyn-bashing BBC. Right wing monsters."

I am not of the school of thought that says, "If you're upsetting everyone you must be getting the balance right." If everyone hates you there is a strong chance you're the problem. But if both sides of a political spectrum think you're on the other side, we might be seeing paranoia.

It's the race to victimhood. If you can be offended by someone's joke you can shut them down. It's wrong from either side but it's hypocritical from the right. Some people spend 12% of their lives complaining, "You can't say anything these days." As soon as they see a left-wing comedian say something they scream, "Not fair, make it stop!"

Finding the right balance in comedy is a Herculean task. The BBC may never reach the sweet spot but it should try. Make more comedy, make more right-wing comedy but don't make less of what you're doing well. You don't achieve balance by taking everything off the see-saw.

If more right-wing comedy is made, the left should hold back from trying to get every show cancelled for saying a thing they disagree with. As long as no laws are being broken, comedy should be allowed.

The BBC shouldn't cower away from holding the Government to account. Comedy will always be anti-establishment and it always has been. After an episode of The Mash Report went out a few series ago I saw someone on social media saying, "It's biased, bring back Spitting Image." Then they did bring it back and people tweeted that it was biased.

Only time will tell if the Telegraph's reporting was correct. When I saw the headline I didn't believe my eyes. So I took a drive to Barnard Castle.

It's OK, that's not a biased joke, he's not a Tory.

Baby Names

Steve is a common name. It's OK, I have made my peace with the fact that it's nothing special. When I went to Priestsic Primary School I was one of 4 Stevens in my class and probably one of thousands in the NG postcodes.

Back then everyone was a Steve. Be it Davis or Hendry you couldn't even win at snooker without joining the Steve club.

The list of new popular baby names has been released again. In 2019, Oliver and Olivia have remained at the top, which shows how uncreative we are. It's basically the same name.

Oliver has been the top of that list for seven years now. Give it a decade and then shout Oliver in a crowded shopping mall and see the mayhem you'll cause.

Chin up, Olivers. I know what it's like to have a common name and if you need a shoulder to cry on just ask a Steve, like we asked the Johns before us.

I am more impressed that we have the list at all. At the start of the lockdown many people predicted another baby boom. If we were all stuck at home, unable to leave and only so many episodes of Tiger King available, the assumption was we'd get up to all kinds of naughty fun. An increase in the birth rate was expected to be nine months down the line.

It looks like we were wrong. There hasn't been a noticeable increase in pregnancies but I saw one news story saying the number of couples applying for a divorce was double what you'd expect.

Having more time together doesn't lead to more romance, it makes us notice what we can't stand about someone.

People thought it would be like the baby boom of the mid-twentieth century but that was fuelled by men coming home from a war. Their wives hadn't seen them in ages and couldn't keep their hands off them. If they had seen their hubbies sitting around the house all day, with their unshaven faces sticking out of their food stained t-shirts, history may have been different.

It's also worth remembering that the post-war baby boom was in a time before the pill was invented. Even if couples passed their lockdown getting friendly it wouldn't always make babies.

Congratulations to you if you are having a post-lockdown baby. I hope you'll have a very happy family life, but when you get to the school gates in a few years' time listen out to how many parents call their children things like, "Miracle," "Longshot" or "Jesus," because it must have been an immaculate conception.

Hard Water

My body is a temple. One that has fallen into disrepair, but a temple nonetheless.

I do not let toxins or impurities enter my body, so imagine my shock when I woke up, checked the Swindon Advertiser website and saw the headline that said Swindon's water could be damaging people's skin.

I was so shocked I spat out my coffee and nearly dropped my cigarette into my burger.

We all know we are supposed to drink two litres of water a day. I'm pretty good at hitting that target because I learned to down pints in my sillier youth and now I use that skill to stay hydrated.

My water habit started a few years ago when I would regularly see the Daily Mail's health section. Every time it would ask something like, "Do you have dry skin?" the solution would be to drink more water. "Do you get headaches?" Drink more water. "Do you want to control your weight?" Drink more water.

Then one day they said, "Could you have diabetes? Have you found yourself going to the toilet more often?" Yes, because you've got me drinking a reservoir a day.

The reason that Swindon's water would be bad for our skin is its hardness. It's chemicals like magnesium and calcium sulphates and phosphates. I thought they were good for me. Calcium is good for my bones and phosphates are good for the garden, so they are probably good for my gut flora.

Thankfully it's not about the hard water you drink, it's the hard water you shower in. The minerals can be left on your skin after washing. It's difficult to know what to do. You can't wash them off with more water, you're just adding to the problem.

And you can't stop washing. That was just a phase in your teenage years.

I have always lived in hard water areas. Descaling the kettle is like a pastime for me. You know how, after you have used the descaler, you have to boil the kettle once more before use? Well I have lived in places where, after that final cleaning boil, the limescale has started to build up again.

That water was so hard, I could never have a water mattress, I'd bruise myself getting into bed.

While the chemicals on our skin can apparently make us look older, if you're like me you have admitted that's what you look like now. I'm getting older. There's no shame in that. Medicine keeps us alive longer than ever before but media tells us we're useless after 25.

Maybe the lesson is, don't mess with our water, it's harder than you think.

School's Back from Summer

Good luck to any children who have gone back to school. I know the schools have gone back because I have seen buses that say, "School Bus," on them, and a new phenomenon of some buses that say, "No School Children," in the window.

It's the kind of segregation I have always dreamed of. It's nice to know I can get on a bus without fear of meeting a large group of young ones playing Cardi B out of their phones.

It's daunting enough to start a new school year. I remember my first day at Sutton Centre. We were all taken into the sports hall and separated into groups. The more I think about it the more it feels like something from The Hunger Games. They were probably hoping for something more like Harry Potter but things were different back then.

I can only imagine what it must be like for the latest cohort entering the next stage of their education during this strange time.

I worried about making friends. It must be even harder when you have to wear a face mask. It's hard to bond with someone when you can't see their face. It's hard to see if they like you if you can't see them smile. And if you do make a friend you may never recognise them again because you only saw their eyes.

We used to worry about bullies. Right now in school the pupils have to worry about catching a virus. My father would say, "Stand up for yourself and fight back. Never start a fight but be ready to finish one."

That advice isn't going to help you fight off a virus. In fact, getting your fists involved in anything will only mean you need more hand sanitiser.

We worried about looking fashionable but we didn't have mask fashion to worry about. I have found a very comfortable mask, which my other half tells me looks like a reinforced gusset. If you wear something like that in school you'd never live it down. Children can be cruel and so can a fiancée, as I have found out. I try to ignore her comments and point out that my mask is comfortable and breathable but she points out, "So are gussets."

Best of luck to you if you're at school. The only advice I can give is to try your best, to work hard, and be nice to your teacher. They might be the ones guessing your exam grades in the future.

Return of the Sequels

Sequels are never as good as the original. It is a fairly robust rule. There are exceptions, but for every Terminator 2 there's a Matrix Reloaded to balance things out.

The first part of a story is the best part. It's where we learn a lot about ourselves and deal with the big issues. In the second part of a story, everything is less impressive. It's why we have eight different films showing Peter Parker turning into Spider-Man.

I mention this because we could be heading into

Lockdown II: The Sequel. After the number of positive tests for Covid increased sharply the Government is bringing in new restrictions.

The first time round it was interesting to see how we'd cope, but this time it feels laborious. They are reducing the number of people you can have in your house from 30 to six.

Firstly, who was having 30 people in their homes? I don't have enough chairs. Even if people are willing to sit on the floor, who has that many cups?

You can't have more than six friends inside your home but you can go to the pub and be inside with many strangers. Why do they think strangers are safer than friends? Have they met my friends?

Is this a ruse to get us all out in the pubs supporting the economy? They have been telling us to get back to work, to school and into restaurants and we haven't all been listening. If they make being at home more boring perhaps we will start to listen to them. It's Sneak Out To Help Out.

I was shocked to hear the Government plan to make it a requirement for all pubs to take the contact details of drinkers. I didn't realise it wasn't before. Why have I been handing out my phone number before a drinking session? It's like trying to pull, but in the wrong order.

I hope they keep an eye on the figures. If the number of cases jumps up but the death rate stays low we should undo these extra measures. Eventually coronavirus could become widespread but non-fatal. We don't shut down the economy to stop people getting cold sores, so let's keep some perspective. We need to balance health worries and the need to live a full life.

I am willing to do whatever it takes to stop another lockdown. I'm bored of stockpiling, working on Zoom and binge-watching Netflix. I've seen all of the good films on there. If we're locked down again I may have to start watching sequels. Argh!

Rule of Six

I visited my father in the care home again recently. I turned up wearing my mask. He didn't know why I had it on but he thought I was wearing it to be silly, which shows that he still remembers what I can be like.

I am trying to get as many visits in as possible because I worry that greater lockdown restrictions will mean I won't be allowed to go again.

We were told that a test and trace system would let us get back to normal. Somehow the people in charge seem to have been taken by surprise that a test and trace system might include some testing. You wait till they work out how much tracing is needed too.

We were promised an app to make the system work but that hasn't happened yet. We seem to have spent the last few years being told that our phones are spying on us and they know too much about us, but as soon as that could be useful we find out it's not as easy as it looks.

Scotland has a version of an app that will track where you have been and with whom. It's like a reverse Tinder; it knows who you have already met and makes it less likely you'll catch something.

We might not need an app to spy on us because so many people are doing it already. There's a heated debate about whether you should report someone if you see them breaking the rule of six.

Would you call the police if you saw someone in a meeting of seven people or more? It's a difficult decision. You don't want to upset them, they outnumber you. If they don't outnumber you, you're breaking the rule too.

Home Secretary Priti Patel has said she would call the police on neighbours for breaking the rules but she'd probably call the police on someone for doing "counter-terrorism", which means she'll have a large phone bill.

I'd probably be willing to snitch if it was like the movies. A detective would ask me what I'd seen, I'd pretend to have a bad memory, he'd offer me money and I'd suddenly remember. In real life it's just being a curtain-twitcher.

It's important to know the details of the rule before you use it on someone. It's not all groups greater than seven that are illegal. The Government has made grouse hunting exempt.

So, if you want to meet up with a lot of friends just take a grouse with you. They can't touch you for it.

Road to Nowhere

I have a terrible thing to confess. I only hope you can find it in the depth of your heart to forgive me. Here goes. I own a car.

It's only a small one. It's so small it's exempt from ULEZ charges and road tax, but it is a car and it feels like drivers are hated.

I say that because recently I parked the tiny Steve-mobile on Downs Road. Don't worry, I wasn't there long. At £11.40 for four hours I can't park there often without my bank texting me.

I tried to drive to Amhurst Road but the road had a new restriction. You may have seen it. It looked like someone had left two large plant pots on the road. I tutted and muttered something about Charlie Dimmock going rogue but I noticed there was a road sign on it.

It's now a dead end for cars. I didn't mind, I simply headed up Benthal Road, but then that was closed off too.

Maury Road was the same. By this time I'd performed so many three-point turns my delts were showing some great definition.

I went up Rendlesham Road planning to use Brooke Road to get onto Evering Road but the phantom road gardener had left more obstacles there. After a little cry I headed back to where I parked, on past the Star and out that way.

I know I should walk, but I'm a stand-up comedian and walking to the gig I had in Haywards Heath would have taken so long I'd miss my stage time.

I am sorry that I'm still driving. I'm sorry I can't e-scooter or whatever, but most of all, I would like to apologise for all of the extra fuel I burned off trying to find a way out.

Do Your Homework Again

Here we go again. It seems like only last week we were being told to get back to work. That's because we were being told that last week. This week we're being told to work from home.

Michael Gove was interviewed on the TV and he called it a, "Slight shift in emphasis." It wasn't that long ago we were told that if we didn't get back into the office we might be easier to sack. Now they're telling us to work from home again. It's less of a slight shift of emphasis and more like a 180° turn.

I'd love to see Michael Gove commentating on rally driving. He would excitedly tell us about the moment the driver pulled up the handbrake as he went round the corner, performing a stunning slight shift in emphasis.

Even if this coronavirus hadn't happened, working from home should be allowed anyway. We don't have to be facing a global pandemic to find a way to spend less of our lives in traffic.

The real problem is that home-workers don't pop into a coffee shop to spend a tenner on a drink and sandwich. Those purchases keep the economy going.

I'll meet the economy halfway. If I am working from home I will recreate a coffee shop experience. I can make my own coffee, I can try to force myself to have a muffin too and then throw seven quid away.

I know it's a shame for the towns. Whenever I go into the centre of Sutton it's sad to see so many shops closed. It looks like Outram Street did a few years ago. I try to remember that if we head back to a full lockdown the situation will be worse and some of those shops will stay closed permanently.

If you went back to work, I am not saying it is your fault. You were putting the effort in and following the advice we were given. Don't lose heart because at some point in the future will we need to have that attitude again.

It feels like a moment where the people who tried to get us back into the office should admit they were wrong but that never happens these days. Politicians insist they were right before and they're right now, even if they're saying the total opposite.

If they get things wrong they deny it. If we get things wrong we risk a £10,000 fine.

I don't know why I'm so angry about working from home. I don't have any work at the moment anyway.

Panic Buying Again

Have you done your panic buying yet? I do most of mine online, and spread it out over a few weeks.

Last week some shops asked people not to panic buy. That was probably the worst thing they could do. As soon as you hear that you think, "Does that mean other people are panic buying? I don't want to be left behind, I'd better pop to the shops for a quick panic buy."

The cynical part of me wonders if some shops are hoping for a little run on some products to boost their sales figures. If they're struggling to shift a certain item, issue a press release asking people to not panic buy it all, and they'll sell more. It's the only reason I have so many tins of sardines. I don't even like sardines.

I thought we learned from last time. When the original lockdown came in a lot of us bought more than we needed. The most highly sought-after product in March was the humble loo roll.

We all saw the news reports of some corner shops charging exorbitant prices for a roll. With the price of toilet roll going up and the pound going down, put it this way, it's a good job they got rid of the one-pound note.

I didn't think I was a panic buyer but even I felt the urge to pick up some spares if I was near the shops. You don't need too many details here but I haven't had to buy any more toilet rolls since then, and I haven't run out of flax seed. That was probably too much detail, wasn't it?

Given that we have so recently been through a panic buying pandemic I expected better from us. The fact that we still have items from the first surge tells us we don't need to do it. We saw images of people working long shifts for the NHS, saving people's lives, going to the shops on the way home and not being able to buy the bare essentials.

No one wants to see that again and we can surely remember that we don't have to be selfish in the shops. It doesn't stop some. I saw a picture of a woman leaving a supermarket with bags of pasta and around 128 rolls. That looks like the picture of someone who doesn't know they're gluten intolerant.

If I can't say, "Don't panic buy!" without causing it, and I can't tell you to panic buy, all I can say is this. I have loads of loo roll left if you need to buy some.

10 OCTOBER

Take My Job, Please

They are coming for our jobs. The mainstream media loves them but don't be fooled, they are taking work away from us.

I am, of course, talking about celebrities.

Channel Four has announced a new two-part TV show where famous people try their hand at stand-up comedy. As a professional stand-up comedian this news doesn't make me feel valued. It is hard enough to feel good about yourself when the Government makes your profession illegal for much of the year.

While the nation's live entertainers have been forced to sit at home regretting having claimed so many expenses on their past self-assessment forms the celebrities have been moving in on our territory.

I have been performing in comedy clubs for over 15 years now. When I first started, the elders of the circuit passed on their wisdom. They told the novitiates the only way to get good at this art form is to put the time in. We have all spent years trying out material to judgemental crowds, eating "meals" in motorway services and giving up the social hours of our lives to learn how to be a stand-up.

Little did we know a sex tape or famous parent would have saved us the trouble.

It feels somewhat insensitive. It is a time when the lockdown has hit our part of the hospitality sector hard, and many talented performers are struggling financially. Every day I hear of a fellow performer who can't afford to stay in the industry. Then a TV show comes along looking at how easily we can be replaced. It's like pitching Celebrity Loom Usage just to rub the Luddites' noses in it.

Media insider types have said that names like Roman Kemp and Vicky Pattison are being bandied around. Roman is a radio host. He has a bit of an advantage. It's like when Strictly Come Dancing pick a former dancer in a pop group. As a radio host you have experience in telling funny stories and hearing no laughter from the audience. Both are crucial skills in the early days of your stand-up career.

As someone who took the long route round I'd like to believe that you can't learn stand-up overnight. It takes experience to know your place on that stage. It takes time to develop the skills of crowd work and delivery.

Stand-up comedy used to be one route to becoming famous. In America the career path of stand-up to sitcom was well trodden. Yet now somehow we're making TV shows where celebrities try to become famous. The world of entertainment is falling in on itself.

Stand-up is often treated badly compared to the other arts. It took a pandemic for the Arts Council to realise we were artists. Would we accept a TV show where someone off EastEnders chanced their arm at fine art or museum curation?

The answer is, yes we would. In fact the first concept has probably been on Sky Arts already and Celebrity Museum may be coming soon to Channel Five.

The problem isn't the celebrities, it's unoriginal pitching. It's true that adding a celebrity to a TV show will make more people tune in and more newspapers write about it. The problem here is our attitude to celebrity.

Logic tells us we should want to watch the finest and most skilful exponents of a discipline do their work. We should want to watch the best stand-ups doing stand-up and the best chefs cooking, but Celebrity Masterchef shows the logic fails somewhere.

It won't be about the comedy. While there will be moments that work, much of the entertainment will come from seeing people try and fail. The same effect that lets us enjoy someone's shower-singing on The X Factor will make us want to see someone from a reality TV show have an on-stage comedic death.

The same would be true of Celebrity Paramedics. It would be the times the celebs accidentally splint the wrong limbs that people enjoy.

If people want to see someone try and fail at stand-up there are enough new acts ready to do that just as soon as we can get audiences back in clubs.

Will this TV format work? Yes. Even I will be sat on my sofa from my pseudo-furloughed position, watching to see how easy it is to put me out of work.

Bye, Cinema

When I was working on the GWR FM breakfast show, one of my favourite things to do with my day was go to the cinema.

I saw some great films in my local Cineworld. I also saw

Star Wars: Revenge of the Sith. If you knew me in person back then, I am sorry for how much I ranted about that film.

Those fond memories have been bubbling up to the surface since I heard the news that the Cineworld cinema chain is set to shut its screens. There are 5,500 jobs put at risk by this move, which is a trickle-down effect of the coronavirus.

During the first lockdown we couldn't go to the cinema so many big titles were held back. You can't release a movie when nobody can go and see it. It would be the cinematic version of a tree falling down in private.

The most famous case of filmic delay was the new Bond film. It's called No Time To Die, which is a really unfortunate title during a pandemic. It would have been insensitive to release it as the numbers were peaking.

The title wasn't the only unfortunate thing about the film. Rami Malek plays a villain who wears a mask, and in the modern world that makes him one of the good guys.

Since then the cinemas have been allowed to reopen but with social distancing and with the audience wearing masks. That will have hit the cinemas' bottom line. Not the social distancing so much, not every screening was a sell-out, but the masks. If you're wearing a mask you can't nibble on popcorn and drink a cola, and at £15 for snacks, that is clearly where the cinemas made their money.

The final straw came when the Bond film was delayed yet again. Is it because the second wave is also a bad time for a film with that title? Just rename the film, guys, or you'll never get to release it.

It is hoped that the Cineworld cinemas will be able to reopen next year, with staff being asked to accept redundancy in the hope of rejoining the company when theatres open again.

It would be a shame to lose this institution. Without the cinema where would couples go on a date when they don't want to have to talk? Where would many people get their first kiss? Where would some of us go to watch a film and cry like a baby? It was Star War: Revenge of the Sith I cried at. I remember blubbing, "That's two hours twenty-six minutes of my life I'll never get back."

Wet Mask Problems

It's an issue that will affect almost all of us yet I haven't heard any so-called experts talking about it.

It's October and that means we can expect some rain. We are also experiencing a pandemic and that means we are wearing face masks. The logical consequence of those two facts is that we're going to get wet masks.

This happened to me recently. I was travelling back from performing at a stand-up comedy gig. I was walking to the bus stop because the curfew meant I wasn't travelling home late and a bus is about the level of glamour I'd better get used to now.

As the heavens opened, I counted myself lucky that I was wearing my winter coat. I hadn't noticed the droplets of rain water slowly absorbing into my disposable mask. A few minutes later it had started to turn into a kind of papier-mâché.

If you want to make a mould of your lower face this is a great trick, but for the rest of us it's bad news. Wet paper doesn't let air through.

There's no official Government advice on what to do if you get a wet mask. Some people have said that even after you dry it off it won't be as effective. That makes sense for the ones made of paper. You can also tell if a book has been dropped in the bath no matter how well you dry it off.

This also means it's a bad idea to soak your paper mask in cold tea to make it look like an old pirate era mask.

A fabric mask you can wash but that doesn't help you in the moment. When you have that wet cloth mask on your face it feels like wearing a damp sock.

I mentioned this issue on social media. I'd like to thank everyone who rushed to point out that a water-proof mask might not be a good idea. You could make one from plastic but you'd find it much harder to breathe. You'd end up blowing most of your air out the sides.

I realise I may be overreacting to a small issue. My bigger point is that there are many little details of the way we're being asked to live our lives that I think the experts should pay attention to.

I was on the busiest bus I've seen in ages because of the curfew-induced kicking out time. People are trying to rush their dessert in a restaurant when their evening was never going to turn into a debauched session.

It's the small details that will make this system succeed or fail.

Trump Got Ill

What is a satirist to do with Trump?

The news that the President of the United States of America has contracted the coronavirus has left some of us in a difficult position.

Even though we have had to see some pretty shocking news in recent years, most of the topical comedians are still human. You know, deep down. When you hear the news of a man in his seventies contracting a virus that can be fatal to people in that age bracket, you have empathy.

Science tells us that the virus is really tough for those who are overweight. Now, some say Donald Trump lies about his height to bring his BMI down but viruses don't check paperwork. It's another reason to show concern for someone who is ill.

If we only listened to the angel popping up on our shoulder, that would be the end of it. But the devil on our other shoulder loves to point out the hypocrisy. When a man who belligerently said the coronavirus would be gone by the summer catches it in the autumn, it's worth a mention.

When someone who recently said publicly that Covid-19 affects "almost no one", how can we not sarcastically say, "So you're calling yourself a no one?"

He held rallies where his supporters defiantly refused to wear a mask. That's because wearing a bit of fabric as a small effort to help everyone else has become a political issue.

It was surprising as Donald has been known as a germophobe for quite some time. Most germophobes would like people to wear masks even when there's no pandemic but the political capital to be gained by making the "do-gooders" seem bad was too tempting. And look where it's got him.

Even the most sympathetic commentator must find irony in the man who said using bleach as a cure is now in a hospital using proper drugs suggested by proper doctors. Trump suggested putting UV light into the body. Did he try putting a sunbed lamp up his botty before trying real drugs?

Just as the poetic irony of the situation starts to entertain there will be a ping on my phone from a news app telling me that doctors say the next 48 hours will be critical for him. That jolts me back to thinking that no matter what point of view someone has held, you shouldn't make light of something that could cost them their lives.

Show sympathy. That can't be wrong. But just as soon as I

start to think that, social media shows me the conspiracy theories that he doesn't actually have Covid and he's only doing this to get out of future debates. His current narrative is that his opponent Joe Biden is old and frail. If Trump can claim to have had a tough case of Covid but walked it off in a few days he can look fit by comparison.

Now I don't want to fall into the trap of giving sympathy if it's not due but I don't want to accuse someone of pretending to be ill in case they go on to die.

There was another conspiracy theory that claimed the President was hiding a secret oxygen tank about his person and using a mask to cover the nose attachment. Several mainstream media outlets have claimed that's nonsense but I remember someone saying those outlets peddled "fake news". I wonder who could have said that?

What about all of those Trump supporters who claimed that coronavirus was a hoax? Do they see the contradiction of their position, or do they think this proves that people can catch made-up illnesses? Be careful what you pretend is real, as some people could catch that. I'm terrified that I might come down with a case of The Phage from Star Trek Voyager.

I haven't noticed many Trump supporters saying sorry for thinking this virus that has killed over one million people was a hoax. They are too busy saying that Trump critics shouldn't mock him. They ask how the left would like it if it was one of their figureheads who got ill. Maybe people replied with the clip of Trump mocking Hilary Clinton after we heard she had pneumonia. Even more hypocrisy.

Donald has been rude about people with illnesses and dismissive of the disease he now has. His actions may well have led to more people catching it. And yet, I still don't want to mock him. He's an old man who is ill.

Donald, get well soon, so we can get back to pointing out what a hypocrite you are.

Three Tiers, Hip Hip...

It's starting to look like I don't have common sense. Maybe I am the kind of person behind the reason they put "do not iron clothes while wearing them" on the box your steam iron came in.

The reason my common sense is in doubt is because our leaders have said time and again that they will rely on the common sense of the British people to enforce the Covid compliance rules. They have also brought in a new tier system, which I am finding confusing. Am I lacking the common sense to understand them?

Firstly, it is a three tier system. I am following so far. What's the lowest tier? It's Medium. I thought if something was medium it had to be between a bigger and a smaller thing. If this Government were in charge of writing the Goldilocks story, the first bear's bed and porridge would have been good enough.

Having the lowest level called Medium makes this feel like someone put Costa coffee in charge. We're lucky the levels aren't medium, large and Venti.

Let's look at the other end of the scale. What's the highest tier? Is it the one called high? No. High is the medium one. Of course it is. The highest is called Very High.

I presume they did this to scare the living daylights out of us. If you call the lower level "low" people might relax. Then why stop there? Call the bottom level "very high", the medium one "really very high" and the highest one "Aaarrgh!" That'll keep us all indoors.

Thankfully Swindon is medium and by that I mean the low medium, not the medium that's high. See, it's not just me, it's a confusing system.

This first tier has the same rules that were in place already. They could have called it the "normal" tier but that would have been too easy.

Tier 2 has stricter rules which mean you can't meet people indoors. Sales of outdoor heaters have already gone up 400%, so we know what Greta will be complaining about next year.

Under tier 2 rules people in relationships who don't live together can't meet up to get intimate indoors. They may head outdoors but it's getting cold. So if you have recently purchased an outdoor heater you may have to wave off more than moths.

The new rules are meant to be easier to understand but it feels like we'll have to look up information on a chart before we leave the house. Does that seem like common sense to you?

Free The Wales

I want to take a look over the border to see what life could be like for us soon. By the border I don't mean we should look to Berkshire, who in their right mind would do that? Head the other way along the M4 and we can learn lessons from Wales.

The Welsh nation is currently trying a circuit breaker lockdown, which for some reason they're calling a firebreak. I don't know if they held a focus group and ascertained that firebreak sounds sexier than the thing that bothers you when you're trying to mow the lawn, but it doesn't matter, it's the same thing.

It would make more sense if Wales was an island because if this firebreak works, as soon as it's lifted, we English can have day trips to Wales again and cough all over the place.

One interesting detail is that shops in Wales have cordoned off the non-essential aisles in the supermarkets. You could buy food and drink, but if you wanted to buy some plates to eat that food from, you were out of luck.

Also prohibited were the sales of clothing from supermarkets. I am not sure how living without new undies for the 17-day period would help but I'm not an expert in public health.

How can they call clothing non-essential, and yet when I try to go out while not wearing any I get asked to leave the bus?

If you have left the house to go into a shop you have created a certain level of risk. What difference does it make what you buy when you're in the shop? In fact handling pots and pans is less risky than checking to see if an avocado is ripe. We can easily wash cookware before we use it but you can't run fruit and veg through the dishwasher. It doesn't come out well, trust me.

I genuinely feel sorry for the people of Wales during this extra lockdown. It feels like they are being used as guinea pigs. They'd better not try that here. We all know the love I have for the massive Asda in the Orbital Shopping Park. If they try to stop me checking out the seasonal aisle I think I'd lose it.

If they prevented me from looking at the TVs I'll never be able to afford, or the cheap smartphones I always think about buying if my track and trace app dobs me in, I'd be outraged.

I'd do what all people who write to newspapers do and I would craft a strongly-worded letter. The only problem is they'd have the stationery aisle locked down. Outwitted again.

11 NOVEMBER

Lockdown 2

Here we are again. I would love to be writing some silly jokes about an obscure news story to give you a giggle, but instead the topic on our minds is the national lockdown.

It feels like it came out of nowhere. I'm annoyed because I spent the last week trying to learn all the rules to the three tiers. It's like doing Duolingo Italian to find out you can only go on holiday to the spare room, which is one of the rules.

I'm glad to see some of the tier rules go. One stated that pubs in tier three could only serve alcohol with a substantial meal. If I lived in tier three I'd be on eight meals an evening.

There are some differences between this lockdown and the first. I hope that by looking at those differences we can spot the ways this time will be easier.

It is Autumn. In the first lockdown we were locked inside while the weather slowly got nicer and taunted us. This time the clocks have already changed and daylight is a rarity. If you want to go sunbathing in the park now, you have bigger issues in your life than a virus.

Meeting indoors or in private gardens will not be allowed, but individuals can meet one other person from another household outside in a public place. I've nominated Santa in case this lockdown lasts longer than planned.

If you know someone who's living on their own you could hire yourself out as company for them. It might be the only way some of us manage to earn any money for the rest of the year.

Lockdown Two hasn't closed the universities. If you really want to get out of the house you could sign up for a degree. In my youth I did chemistry at uni, so I'd recommend that. I had a friend who did a history degree. He had so few lectures if you did that course you'd still feel like you were in lockdown.

This time we are not limited to only one hour of exercise a day. I never went over that before and I won't this time either but it is nice to know we have that freedom.

The main difference, in which there's hope, is that we are older and wiser. We have lived through a lockdown. We know what to do. We know not to panic buy, we can work Zoom and we have already seen Tiger King on Netflix.

We know we can do this. If we stick together and look out for one another it'll be over in no time.

Feeling The Stress

It has been a strange time lately. As if we didn't have enough to worry about, bird flu came back to the UK. Some farms including one over the border in Kent had cases. It seems so old school in comparison to coronavirus, almost retro.

I'm keeping away from any pigs because swine flu must be getting jealous. The same is true for Spanish flu, so I will also keep away from any Spaniards.

Those news stories added to the anxiety we were all feeling. Over the last week I have had the pleasure of presenting some shows on Time 107.5 and I have spoken to many callers. There's a general feeling of being sick of it.

One caller told me the effort they had to put in to get a haircut. They had worked out that it was the last chance to get a trim before doing so became illegal again. The first lockdown was extended a few times so you can't be sure when your next haircut will be.

I think that's a good way to measure lockdowns, what will we look like when it's over. Are we talking a Ken Barlow fringe from the 80s? Will we look like a footballer from the 70s? Or will it be the full Tom Hanks in Castaway? We need to know.

As ever, I am here to look on the bright side. As we start a second lockdown, remember that it will lower the odds of you getting Covid as well as bird flu, swine flu or a cold. And having hair that makes you look like something escaped from a zoo will make you feel like isolating more. So don't let the anxiety get to you, it'll all work out in the end.

Captain Tom

Captain Sir Thomas Moore has done it again. You may know him as the winner of The Best Thing About 2020. Admittedly, there wasn't a lot of competition. He only had to be better than Tiger King on Netflix and sour dough bread to be crowned the winner.

In the first lockdown Captain Tom, as he was then, raised £33million for the NHS by walking 100 laps of his garden. It was an inspiring act especially when you remember he was just about to turn 100 years old.

His attitude and spirit spread. He gave us an uplifting news story when we really needed it. He also took away our excuse to be idle. If he could do a sponsored walk we could all get off the sofa and stop feeling sorry for ourselves.

Now we have a second lockdown we have a second effort from Sir Tom. He has launched a new walking challenge. He wants to get people walking to help support those who feel lonely and frightened during lockdown.

His challenge encourages people to log their walking activity on social media using the hashtag #WalkWithTom. The genius of this is that it will be similar to all of the social media posts you see from people who have taken up running but it will be far less annoying.

Most days my Twitter is full of red faced sweaty people boasting about how quickly they did a 5k. Some of them helpfully post a map of their route so we know where to avoid.

Boastful joggers also help with the issue of loneliness, in that seeing their Instagram photos of them in Lycra makes me happy to be on my own.

Tom's plan comes at exactly the right time. For those of us who have lost a relative this year the bereavement can be hard to cope with but knowing that we're all coming together to offer support can help.

Good luck to you if you are taking part or even if you are making sure that your neighbours, friends and relatives aren't left feeling lonely. If you're waving through the window to say hi, like I have to with my elderly Dad, or if you're walking round some shopping and talking through someone's letter box, well done you.

The only thing that Sir Captain Tom hasn't mentioned is that the weather isn't as good as when he did his walk. So wrap up. Not all heroes wear capes but they should wear a scarf and gloves.

Burgers

We are often told to eat better food. Public information films tell us to swap snacks for fruit. Sugary drinks have tax put on them. Chocolate bars were made smaller but then sold in twin packs, so that was a waste of time.

After all of this relentless nagging it is nice to see a news story that tells us to tuck into some naughty food. We have been told to get out there and buy food from McDonald's. The really surprising thing is we were told to do it by Burger King.

The regal fast food place posted on social media saying, "Order from McDonald's. We never thought we'd be asking you to do this."

It came as a surprise to me. I expected to hear it was the brainchild of the new Burger King employee, who has bright red hair, a white face and goes by the name Ronald.

Had they all run out of burgers or something? I couldn't think of another reason for Burger King to advertise a competitor. They also mentioned KFC, Subway, Greggs and other outlets. I started to think it was the actions of someone on their last day. We all dream of doing something like that. For every time the boss has been annoying we have developed plans for revenge.

They claim they are trying to help support the whole sector. There are thousands of people employed by these food places and without support there will be job losses. I still don't understand why that's bad for Burger King though.

If they become the purveyor of burger products there will be queues round the block to get their goods, especially at pub closing time, which is a thing again now. And if top chefs, if that's what we call them, from fast food places are looking for work, Burger King will be able to hire the cream of the crop.

When I noticed the link between the shops they mentioned, I wondered if there was a reason Burger King didn't want us weaning ourselves off junk food. If we have another lockdown without this kind of food, will we have broken our addiction? No wonder they're willing to send us to their competitors.

However, it looks like it was all above board. There have been no retractions or repudiations. The King wants you to buy your fast food from its competitors. Before I headed to Greenbridge Retail Park to help out, it struck me. This is probably about getting free advertising.

That act of beefy altruism has led to more people talking about Burger King. I'm doing it right now by typing this. They fooled us all with their Whopper.

Vaccine News

Even though I used to work in a laboratory in Huthwaite before my switch to broadcasting, and even though I am a rational person, I'm still superstitious sometimes. It doesn't cost much effort to knock on some wood or to walk round a ladder, so why not?

That's why I don't want to get too excited about the Covid vaccine that has been developed by Pfizer. I don't want to get my hopes up in case they are dashed yet again, but things are looking good.

The pharmaceutical company has reported the results of their trials show the vaccine is 90 per cent effective, which is more effective than most of us have been since March.

There are plans to see it being used in December. It doesn't mean we'll be back to normal right away, which is fine by me. I don't want to lose my excuse for not shopping a lot this Christmas. This vaccine has come along at the right time to let me put money in Christmas cards this year but we could get our lives back in the spring.

We still have to think about side effects. The drugs company Pfizer is famous for making Viagra but it was originally tested as a heart drug. The drug's raunchier physical impact was an accidental side effect. What if this vaccine has a similar side effect? It would cure the pandemic but we'd still not be able to leave the house.

There is already much discussion about who should get the vaccine first. I know I am biased but I'd say it should go to people in care homes so I can visit my dad again without it feeling like I'm window shopping.

I'm relatively fit and healthy and I tested positive for the antibodies a little while back, so someone like me shouldn't be anywhere near the front of the queue.

The people I think should have to wait the longer are the people who have been posting anti-science memes on social media. When you go for the jab the doctors could check people's Twitter and Facebook. If they have previously said coronavirus is all Bill Gates' fault or posted a picture of the Jackson 5 saying, "Don't blame it on the sunshine, blame it on the 5G," back of the queue for you. Hand them some lavender and a crystal and wish them the best of luck.

As unscientific as it is, I'll be keeping my fingers crossed that this vaccine can restore some normality to our lives. Fingers crossed, but also washed for 20 seconds while singing Happy Birthday.

Christmas Ads

Many Christmas traditions will have to sit this year out. We may not be allowed an office party. Kissing under the mistletoe will be verboten. Even pulling a cracker might be tricky if we have to stay two metres apart. A company could clean up if they made crackers that were two metres long. And if you do, remember where you got the idea and please send me 10 per cent of the profits.

One tradition that we can do from a distance is watch the Christmas adverts from certain stores. The most anticipated one is the John Lewis ad. Seeing as the John Lewis At Home store in the Mannington Retail Park was a victim of 2020, if you're not going to pop to the Designer Outlet, watching their advert could be as close to shopping there as we can do.

In the past their adverts have included a man who lives on his own on the moon. In the advert a little girl sends him a telescope. Not a ticket back or a way to communicate, but a telescope so that he can see other people having fun in greater clarity and feel even more isolated.

Another year their advert showed us animals jumping up and down on a garden trampoline, letting us glimpse the future after humanity has fallen. Merry Christmas.

Last year's featured a dragon which accidentally set fire to things in an olden day village where most buildings were made of wood. Forget the Yuletide spirit, health and safety says they should have banished him.

I remember the advert with the boy who woke up early one Christmas to carry a gift to his parents in a cardboard box. He looked like a young Dominic Cummings leaving Downing Street.

For 2020 the advert mixes different styles of live action and animation to show people being helpful. From a girl helping a boy get a football down from a tree to a lady on a bus fixing someone's broken spectacles.

It is possibly the nicest message an advert has ever tried to get across. Sure, its main purpose is to get us to spend money, but that's true of all adverts. This one is also saying be kind to people.

Start small. We could try not honking our car horns at people who don't pull off at the lights as quickly as we'd like. Try not tutting if someone takes a little bit longer to find their purse at the till.

We could graduate to helping short people reach top shelves and lifting prams up stairs. Be nice, it's Christmas. Not long till January when we can go back to being grumpy.

I'm A Grinch

The news that pandemic restrictions will be eased for Christmas has been met with joy by many. We will be able to form bubbles that last for five days, which is impressive for a bubble. We will be free to see members of our extended families.

Sadly there are experts saying these freedoms will come at a price, with some estimating each day with our families could mean five more days of lockdown after. Other experts have spoken more bluntly saying that spending time together over the festive period will cause more deaths.

This made me realise what Wiltshire needs. We could do with some miserable Grinch who can put us off Christmas. Someone who can complain about the small stuff and get more people to spend less time with their loved ones this year. It would reduce the risks.

This could be what I have been training for all these years. I thought I was becoming a grumpy old man before my time, but I was honing my misanthropic skills for when I was called upon.

If I can inspire just one person to think, "We'll leave a day early," I'd be saving lives. So here goes.

Great, they are letting us have extended support bubbles for Christmas. Firstly, I cannot believe they didn't call them

"Support baubles." Sometimes I despair at our leadership.

It doesn't matter how big a bubble we're allowed, there will be some family members who don't get invited. What an efficient way to cause family tensions. It's good to know what the rows at Christmas 2021 will be about already.

You can't meet up with family without taking a gift. The queues in the shops at Christmas can be a nightmare and normal shopping has been heavily queue-based in 2020. Those effects will multiply, therefore if you want to get a gift you'd better join a queue now. You'll be camping outside shops like a Harry Potter fan just to get an in-law some socks.

If you sit out this Christmas, you'll meet up with your various uncles and cousins after Brexit has been sorted and Trump has left the White House. There will still be some alcohol-fuelled gammon vs snowflake style stand-offs at the end of 2021 but at least it won't be the same old topics you've been rowing about for the last four Christmases.

Maybe my attempts to be a Scrooge and inspire humbug might not make you cancel plans but if you were feeling pressure to meet up when you don't feel comfortable doing so, send your family this column and they might give you an easier time.

Happy Gwyneth Season

It was this time last year when I got to write one of my favourite columns. At the end of an election period that saw people rowing on social media and Prime Ministers hiding in fridges it was really nice to write about something as ridiculous as the kind of things Gwyneth Paltrow sells.

This year has been another struggle so it is with pleasure that I can confirm Gwynnie has launched her Goop website Christmas campaign. Let's have a look to see what you can buy from her site to increase your wellness, which seems to be the keyword on there. I'm feeling 'weller' already.

For just £160 you can buy a lamp made out of a real baguette. Don't buy me that as a gift. I tried the Atkins diet once and I'd have had that lamp by day three.

They say there's nothing like the smell of warm bread to help sell your house during a viewing. This lamp must help with that, right before it catches fire and takes your home with it.

Thankfully the bread is coated in resin and it only uses LED bulbs for safety. It's the best thing since sliced bread, which Gwyneth will probably try to sell you for £300 to tile the bathroom.

While we're in the bathroom, her website sells hand and foot rests so that couples can get frisky in the shower. I can't help thinking it would ruin the mood. "You get undressed, I'll go and get the handles and stirrups. We don't want an accident, now do we?"

Romping in the shower is a little like parkour. If you don't think you can do it without falling down you shouldn't even try.

Last year she offered a candle that smelled of a rather intimate part of her. It cost £75. I seem to remember telling you how to make one yourself for much less.

This year Gwyneth has a candle that says on it, "This candle smells like my prenup." As anyone who has been through a divorce will say, there's nothing more terrifying than smelling your prenup burning. Other than what she made the last one smell like, I suppose.

For just under £800 you could get her gemstone therapy map where you lie on some rocks that will make you feel better. I don't know what you'd be feeling bad about. Maybe having spent £800 to lie on pebbles.

With economic uncertainty just around the corner, it might not be the year to waste money on items that no one needs, but thanks to Gwyneth we now know we're not missing out on much.

12 DECEMBER

The Scotch Question

Who would have thought that the biggest question in the Covid lockdown debate would be about the humble Scotch egg? Does it count as a substantial meal? Some pubs will only be allowed to serve alcohol if you're eating a meal, and would eating a Scotch egg mean you qualify?

I must admit, as a stand-up comedian, I have eaten at most motorway services in the UK and the idea that a Scotch egg wasn't a meal shocked me. If it isn't a substantial meal then how come I am so fat? Riddle me that, science.

We debated this issue on the drivetime show on Time 107.5 recently; the hotbed of serious discussion. One caller pointed out that if you had a date, offered to take them out for a meal and just gave them a Scotch egg you'd be going home alone.

Meanwhile another wise correspondent noted that a Scotch egg has the same constituent parts as a sausage and egg sandwich (breadcrumbs are almost as good as bread) and that would definitely be a meal.

I can understand why the Government is in a pickle over this. If they say the egg counts then pubs will buy a job lot from the supermarket and hand them out with pints. People will still have a big session and wake up saying, "I overdid it on the Scotch last night. Not whisky, eggs."

If the Government say a Scotch egg doesn't meet the standards, the SNP will say it's more evidence of Westminster bias and call for another referendum.

We're missing the bigger issue here. If a Scotch egg isn't substantial then someone should have a word with those posh restaurants where you get a mouthful of quail next to three bits of lettuce and they charge you £20.

Vaccination Protestation

We have a vaccine. This is the best news I have heard in ages. It will hopefully mean that I can go to visit my father in the care home without having to shout through a window again and I can go back to travelling the UK to do stand-up.

When the pandemic is over I might keep the mask. I have learned to keep my eyes looking like they are smiling while I can gurn on the lower half and no one can tell.

The UK is the first country to approve a vaccine. This led to the MP Gavin Williamson saying that we're better than other countries. We may well be, but not because we're good at paperwork. Just because you do something fast doesn't mean you're the best. A lot of people read his comments and felt sorry for Mrs Williamson.

Just when I was thinking that nothing could spoil the good vaccine news, along came the antivaxxers. It's a curious mindset. I'm convinced that if the Titanic disaster was to happen now there'd be a group of people on the ship who identify as anti-life-boaters.

I see how it's enticing to feel that you know more than the

experts without the study. I know how it can happen. I have watched all the series of House and started to feel like I was a doctor, but I'm not.

It is a mixture of issues that has caused such a large movement against vaccination. Most of us haven't lived in an era where we saw the effects of things like Measles or Smallpox. It's the paradox of a good vaccination campaign; the better it works, the less people will notice it.

The internet has made it possible for any idea to seem as valid as actual science. I might start a conspiracy theory that the virus was created by Zanussi. Why else would we have a vaccine that has to be stored at -70°C?

When so many scientists are saying that vaccines work but one scientist disagrees, the antivaxxers think that proves their point. If I am on stage and no one in the audience laughs at a joke apart from just one guy sat at the back, that doesn't mean that guy is right.

The little pro-vaccine tweets I have recently made have attracted some angry replies. I know I could stop posting such things but I think it's better that antivaxxers get annoyed at little tweets from me so that they can build up a tolerance for when they meet me in real life. If only there was a way of describing that principle.

Naughty, Not Nice

Are celebrities better than the rest of us? It certainly feels like they think they are when we read about recent cases of the rich and famous breaking the Covid rules.

The singer Rita Ora threw herself a 30th birthday party in London, which broke the lockdown rules. To make things worse she should have been self-isolating after performing in Egypt.

While she called it a small get-together there were 30

people in attendance, which would only have been allowed if it were a funeral. Depending on who had the virus, give it time.

Then we were shocked that the Sky News presenter Kay Burley visited a restaurant in London with nine other diners to celebrate her 60th birthday. She also used a different restaurant's bathroom after the 11pm curfew. More people would be forgiving of that second infraction. I'm not 60 and even I have to plan journeys making sure there are water closets nearby just in case.

It's claimed she then headed to her Knightsbridge home to party on with people from different households.

She partied harder than Rita, who's a pop star and almost exactly half her age. There's no way Kay didn't know the rules. She reads them out at work once every 15 minutes.

At least Rita could claim she never did a song called Rule of Six.

The UK isn't alone in this. In America, Kylie Jenner visited a friend despite California's shelter-in-place order. So it feels like the issue here is fame. Why do famous people think the rules don't apply to them?

While the rest of us are dutifully cramming in a Scotch egg with every pint, the people with higher status act as if they can do what they want.

Celebs have a rich tradition of rule-breaking. In the 1960s famous rebels would set fire to guitars on stage or trash a hotel room. That was different though. The rebellious act was more of a protest, and back then TVs had cathode ray tubes in them so if you could get that out of a window you deserved some praise.

The modern examples of breaking rules weren't done as a statement to make society question its norms. They were done in secret and only came out by accident. The issue here is entitlement.

If you work in an industry that is synonymous with demanding puppies in your dressing room, or having runners to fetch your pretentious coffee, you'll start to feel special.

It's also worth remembering that these cases were linked to big birthdays. Everyone feels more entitled around their birthday. You may have done it yourself, saying, "You want ME to do the dishes? But it's my birthday!" We act like the fact the Earth has done a lap means we should be treated like a prince or princess.

The multiplying effect of a birthday on a celebrity's entitlement means it's no surprise the rules went out of the window, like an old TV.

We have to hope this doesn't make more people think, "Why should I have to stick to the rules if they're not?" That's now known as a Dominic Cummings moment.

What can we do about all this? Rita Ora offered to pay a fine before she was even asked to pay one. All that shows is a monetary fine is no deterrent to the rich and famous.

I learned that lesson at school. When I was doing my GCSEs I saw a fellow pupil break a pipette in a science lesson. When the teacher spotted it the student said, "It's not my fault, you idiot."

The teacher had a knowing smile as he said, "You'll have to pay £8 for the breakage. I would have let you off but it's £8 for the insult."

The pupil replied, "OK, have £16, you fat ****!"

I don't know where that student ended up, but wherever he is, I bet he had a big birthday this year.

See You For Christmas

I have a plan for next year. I invite you to join me. Next

summer I will have a Christmas, because this one seems to have gone to pot. Thanks to the last minute change of rules most people will be seeing relatives on Skype or Zoom to say they are staying at home, or they will be seeing relatives on Skype or Zoom from the car saying they're stuck in traffic and won't make it.

We should have seen it coming. Just a few days before Christmas was cancelled, the Prime Minister said it would be "inhuman" to ban Christmas. It reminded me of that period in politics when David Cameron would give his full support to whichever minister was caught in a scandal just 24 hours before they had to resign.

Why not delay Christmas 2020? Other people get to delay things. Train companies, the makers of the new Bond film and whoever was meant to be delivering my PlayStation 5 all get to do it.

There's no pointing planning for early next year. The vaccine rollout won't have made much impact by then. Depressingly, even if the Government manage to vaccinate one million people per week, it would still take almost two years to vaccinate the UK.

I say we hold Christmas 2020 in the summer. It's better for reducing the spread of respiratory infections, we could have Christmas dinner in the back garden and wrapping paper must be very cheap at that time of year.

I had always wondered what it was like for Australia having Christmas in the hottest month. We could sample what it's like. It would be bad news for anyone dressing up as Father Christmas with a big fake beard, and the snowmen are done for, but for the rest of us it could be fun.

The actual Father Christmas might not be happy either. With the longest day occurring in June he'd have fewer hours of dark in which to deliver all the gifts but I'm sure he could manage it. He might prefer sneaking down people's chimneys when there's no chance of a fire being lit at the bottom of it.

There's no reason to have Christmas in December. Many experts say the religious festival happened then to usurp a Pagan festival. We'd have to change some songs. Nat King Cole wouldn't mention "Jack Frost nipping at your nose" but, "Sunburn's peeling off your nose," would fit in its place.

Best of all, if you don't like your gifts in the summer version of Christmas, you only have six months to wait for more.

Oops! I Did It Again

I have another apology to give. As we were heading towards the end of this difficult year I thought to myself, "At least things can't get any worse." Oops.

I honestly thought we were nearly home and dry. We have a handful of days left and a tight three-tier system in place to keep us healthy.

Many of the risks were gone. There were no works Christmas parties this year. That meant there were no opportunities to spread COVID or be caught in the stationery cupboard with the head of accounts. As someone who is self-employed I get to boast that I am my own boss, but it means I have to throw my own Christmas party and take myself into a store room for a snog. It's less fun than it sounds.

I should have known better than to tempt fate in 2020. Sure enough, I was proved wrong. I promise I won't do it again.

Christmas is all but cancelled because of the new strain of coronavirus. Our five days of Christmas have been cut to just one. The experts say we should keep those Christmas

Day visits to a minimum. That will happen naturally because the weight of traffic on the 25th will probably be huge. We'll spend most of the day trapped in our cars, which is COVID secure. Maybe that was their plan all along.

The new mutation spreads more easily. They make it sound like a margarine. It's also fat-free with no added sugar and high in protein, but so are all viruses.

I don't want to anthropomorphise the coronavirus, because he wouldn't like it, but it feels like the virus heard about the vaccines and decided to up its game.

It would have been easier if the Government cancelled Christmas weeks ago. It still would have been a sad situation but we wouldn't have ordered all the extra food. At least the leftover turkey will act as a stockpile for the inevitable January lockdown.

It's the disappointment that hurts. I once heard a radio host doing a competition to win £1,000. That sounds great, doesn't it? In the link between the songs the presenter said, "Up next we're giving you the chance to win one million… I mean, one thousand pounds."

All of a sudden winning a grand seems like small change. The promise of something better ruins what we actually get. The promise of a joyful and united Christmas makes living without one even harder.

My thoughts are with you as we get through Christmas and here's to a better 2021. Surely it couldn't be worse than this year. Oops! I've done it again.

ABOUT THE AUTHOR

STEVE N ALLEN is a stand-up comedian and radio host. You can also see him on the newsdesk section of BBC2's The Mash Report.
The previous books *Lasted Another Year* and *Lasted Yet Another Year* are available in ebook and paperback. Find out more at mrstevenallen.co.uk

Printed in Great Britain
by Amazon

About the authors

Patrick Dunleavy is Professor of
include *Developments in British*
Choice and *Prime Minister, Cabi*

Helen Margetts is Lecturer in P
Turning Japanese? and is currentl
technology in central government

Stuart Weir is Senior Research Fe
Audit. His latest book, *The Thre*
political freedom in the UK is the

Contents

Executive Summary

1: The New Assemblies' Vo

2: Electing the Scottish Parliament   10

3: Electing the Welsh Assembly   17

Scenario 2. People instead vote for candidates at local level and for parties at regional level in line with their responses in our survey, so that a significant minority of people can engage in 'ticket-splitting'.

Our results span the range of possible outcomes if people's alignments at the time of the Assembly elections stayed the same as they were in May 1997 (see Table 1). Under Scenario 1 the Labour and Conservative parties will both do well, partly because the system used for counting votes tends to favour larger parties over small ones (especially in Wales, where there are fewer 'additional member' seats to correct parties' being over-represented in winning local seats).

But under Scenario 2 voters will behave differently in the devolved assembly elections, casting fewer votes for Labour and the Conservatives and more votes for the Scottish National Party and Plaid Cymru respectively, a powerful effect which will create much more multi-party legislatures than the Labour government at Westminster expects.

Table 1: Summary table of parties' seats under two scenarios

Seats in Scottish Parliament	Con	Lab	LibDem	SNP	Other	Total
Scenario 1: 1997 votes	22	62	16	29	0	129
Scenario 2: Survey responses	13	58	21	37	0	129
Seats in Welsh Assembly	Con	Lab	LibDem	PC	Other	Total
Scenario 1: 1997 votes	13	37	6	4	0	60
Scenario 2: Survey responses	10	35	7	8	0	60

In Wales Labour would have a majority of Assembly members under either scenario, and a single-party Executive controlled by Labour seems to be the most likely governing outcome. In Scotland Labour would be three seats short of the 65 needed to control the assembly on scenario 1, and seven seats short on the basis of survey responses. A Labour-Liberal Democrat coalition executive seems the overwhelmingly likely outcome under either configuration of seats. If the Scottish Parliament follows Westminster practice then the Scottish National Party would clearly emerge as the 'official' opposition party, with all the advantages that this normally implies. Such an outcome is especially likely under our survey scenario when the Conservatives' MSPs would amount to only just over a quarter of the SNP's representation.

In Wales the Assembly seems likely to imply no great change in the party system, which will continue to be structured on the current lines of Labour vs the rest ('the rest' being the Tories, the Liberal Democrats or Plaid Cymru in different areas of Wales). But in Scotland an increasing divide may open up between a Scottish party system and UK politics. In Edinburgh, the increasingly convergent Labour and Liberal Democrat parties could between them command permanent majority support and control 'the establishment', while the SNP is the major opposition, with the Scottish Conservatives pushed to the sidelines. But for Westminster elections the Conservatives would remain the main opposition, and the SNP could continue to confront its traditional difficulties in winning seats on the wider stage.

1: The New Assemblies' Voting System

Both the Scottish parliament and the Welsh Assembly will be elected using a method known as the *additional member system* (AMS). Here voters cast *two* 'X' votes for different types of MP - one vote for a local constituency MP, and one to determine the 'additional members' allocated at regional level (that is across a group of constituencies) to make the outcome proportional. People can vote for the same party across the two levels, or for two different parties, as they choose. But they can only choose one candidate for the local area, and one party to back at regional level. Unlike some other electoral systems, AMS only counts first preferences, and not second or third preferences.

The AMS ballot paper in both countries will be quite similar to existing ones, except that it will have two sections - the first for choosing candidates to represent local constituency seats elected in exactly the same way as first past the post. But the second part of the ballot paper is rather different from anything that British voters have seen before. At the regional

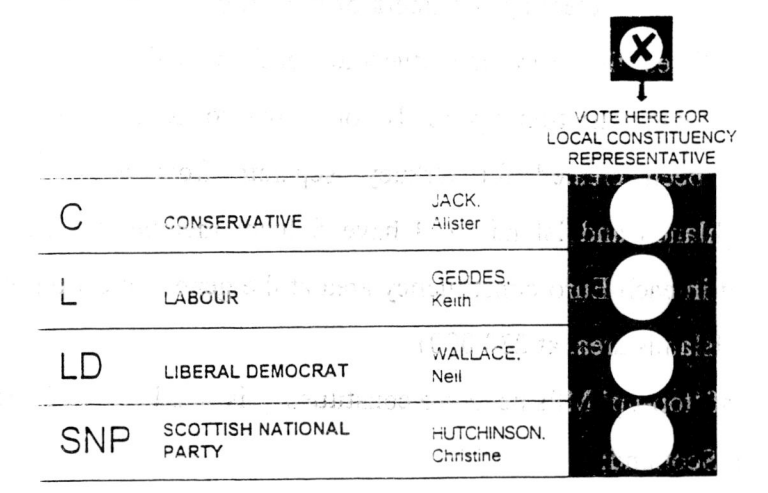

Figure 1

level they can only choose between parties, each of which will put up a list of candidates, presumably with the most popular (or most powerful) party figures at the top of each list. As a party becomes entitled to an additional member seat, so the first person on its list is deemed elected, and the process goes on working down the list in sequence. Figure 1 shows the alternative ballot form we used when ICM asked respondents in Scotland and Wales to vote as if they were voting for the assembly elections. Something like this form will probably be used in the new elections.

In order for parties to offer lists, for the first time in mainland Britain the parties will have to be officially registered, as they are in every country of continental Europe. Once registered the party will be accorded recognition by the British state for the purposes of awarding additional member seats. The state and the law courts need to know, for example, who in the party has the legitimate authority to define its lists of candidates in each region.

Under both the Scottish and Welsh systems the local level is defined as the existing Westminster constituencies. And the 'regional' level for both nations is defined as the current Euro-constituencies, (used for electing Members of the European Parliament in Strasbourg). In both Scotland and Wales the Euro-constituencies each include around nine Westminster constituencies (with some variation up to 10 or down to seven. Since an extra Scottish Parliament seat has been created for Orkney, separate from Shetland Islands the Euro constituency for Highlands and Islands will have 8 local members). Between 280,000 and 400,000 people voted in each Euro-constituency area at the general election in 1997 (with fewer in the Highlands and Islands area, at 230,000).

The number of 'top-up' MPs per Euro constituency is standardized in each country:

- at seven in Scotland;
- but only four additional members in Wales.

As a result the combined number of both local and additional members per Euro-constituency area will be between 11 and 13 in Wales, and much larger, between 15 and 17 in Scotland.

When the votes are counted, the seven top-up seats in Scotland and four top-up seats in Wales are distributed between parties in a complex 'corrective' way, so that parties end up with an overall seats share (across each Euro-constituency and hence across the country as a whole) which is designed to match their share of the vote. Thus a party with 30 per cent of the vote, which had already won 30 per cent or more of the region's seats in local constituency contests would get no additional member seats; while a party which had piled up a lot of votes coming second or third in local constituencies, without winning there, would be compensated with additional members.

The outcome should thus be a Scottish Parliament or a Welsh Assembly where most MPs were locally elected, but where each party's share of seats matches its vote share, thereby yielding a 'proportional' result. However, because the Scottish system has more top-up seats per Euro-constituency there is no room for doubt that it will be considerably more proportional than the system in Wales.

The balance between local members and additional members also varies across the two countries. In Scotland only just over half (57 per cent) of the Parliament will be local MSPs, and over two fifths (43 per cent) of elected representatives will be the additional members. In Wales the local members of the Assembly will account for two thirds (67 per cent), and the additional members for only one third. There is hence a risk in Wales that one party could be so radically over-represented in the local seats that there would not be enough top-up seats to go round. For example, suppose that Labour won 50 per cent of the votes across Wales but by dint of getting their votes in the right places, or because of an evenly fragmented opposition, they gained 38 out of the 40 local seats. Labour would then have 63 per cent of the Assembly seats outright, and the allocation of additional members to the other parties could not redress this imbalance. Such an outcome may seem unlikely - after all, in the 1997 general election Labour gained nearly 62 per cent of the Wales vote, but won only 34 out of the 40 Welsh constituencies. But it is important to recognize that the possibility exists, in a way that Scotland's much more proportional system would not permit.

There are also two minor reasons why both the AMS systems will not be exactly proportional. Very small parties (winning less than five per cent of the vote) may pile up minority support in many areas but never win election in any local seat or at regional level - just as the Referendum Party and others gained 4.4 per cent of the vote in Britain in the 1997 election but no seats. This problem is present in all electoral systems. Second, the pattern of constituencies may not exactly match the distribution of population, with remoter country areas in the far north of

Scotland over-represented somewhat. But this small price has traditionally been one that public opinion is willing to bear in recognition of these areas' distinctive character and problems.

As used in Germany, the AMS system has always had a formal 'threshold' - a level of support which a party must win nationally to gain the right to hold any seats. There is no such formal threshold in either the Scottish or Welsh system. Nevertheless, there is an informal threshold, defined by 100% divided by the overall number of seats in each Euro-constituency. In Scotland that means that a party must win at least six per cent support or more (100/15) in a Euro-constituency to gain a seat, and in Wales as much as nine per cent (100/11). Translated into votes, in the average Euro-constituency, if turnout is as high as it was in the 1997 general election, a party will need to gain 16,500 to 20,000 votes to be sure of winning a seat. This informal threshold is a challenging one - and only the most established and best organized parties are likely to meet it. Hence there would seem to be little present danger of the election of either extremist candidates (for example, for racist parties) or of 'fringe' or non-serious candidates.

A great deal of attention will focus on how parties choose candidates for their lists. The major parties will certainly include at the Euro-constituency level most of the candidates who are standing in each of that area's component local constituencies. A candidate who wins at local level cannot also win an additional member seat - instead the next candidate on the party list (not already elected at local level) will gain the top-up seat. The rules in Wales (which look likely to apply also in Scotland) will prevent any name being included on a party list in more than one Euro-constituency area.

With this background we can move on to seeing how the outcomes would have worked out in practice.

2: Electing the Scottish Parliament

The new Scottish Parliament will have 71 local seats identical with the constituencies used for Westminster elections, plus two more made by splitting up Orkney from the Shetland Islands, 73 in all. There will be 56 additional members, seven each for the Scottish Euro-constituencies. To get a baseline for how this system would work we can take the general election results for Scotland in 1997. Hence all the local seats would go to the parties which currently hold the equivalent Westminster seat. (For Orkney and Shetland we have assumed that the Liberal Democrats would win both seats, since they are the current incumbents of the combined seat).

To see how things would pan out with the additional members we need to add up the 1997 votes in each Euro-constituency and then follow through the slightly complicated AMS procedure for allocating these top-up seats. Table 2 shows an example for the Scotland Mid and Fife Euro-constituency. In the top row we show the combined votes (the party vote) each party gained across the whole area, and below that the number of seats the party has already won in the local constituencies. We now proceed by adding 1 to the local seats, and then dividing the party vote by the resulting figure - for instance, 7 for Labour and 3 for the SNP, 1 for the Tories and 2 for the Liberal Democrats. Scanning across this first division row we see that the Tories have the highest total, so they gain the first additional member. Now we repeat the process for the second division, where all the divisors stay the same except that the Tories have one more seat, so their divisor is now 2: again we scan the row, and this time the SNP has the highest number of votes, so they gain the second additional member. And so the process goes on another five times, by which time the SNP and the Conservatives have won three additional member seats each, the Liberal Democrats have won one, and Labour (already handsomely represented from the constituency contests) has won none. The bottom row shows the final result, which is broadly proportional to the party votes.

This way of allocating seats by division, known to experts as the d'Hondt system after its inventor, has its critics. Usually it tends to favour the largest parties, but in this case because the overall constituency size is large, and there are almost as many top-up seats as local seats, the system works quite fairly. No system of seat allocation is ever completely fair, because in each area there are only so many seats available for distribution. But with 9 local seats and 7 top-up

Table 2: How the AMS system would work in Scotland, using the 1997 results for the Scotland Mid and Fife Constituency

	Labour	SNP	Conservative	Liberal Dem	Additional member result
Party vote	*146,988*	*92,901*	*77,495*	*46,436*	
Local seats	**6**	**2**	**0**	**1**	
1st division	/7 = 20,998	/3 = 30,967	/1 = 77,495	/2 = 23,218	Con wins
2nd division	/7 = 20,998	/3 = 30,967	/2 = 38,748	/2 = 23,218	Con wins
3rd division	/7 = 20,998	/3 = 30,967	/3 = 25,832	/2 = 23,218	SNP wins
4th division	/7 = 20,998	/4 = 23,225	/3 = 25,832	/2 = 23,218	Con wins
5th division	/7 = 20,998	/4 = 23,225	/4 = 19,374	/2 = 23,218	SNP wins
6th division	/7 = 20,998	/5 = 18,580	/4 = 19,374	/2 = 23,218	LDem wins
7th division	/7 = 20,998	/5 = 18,580	/4 = 19,374	/3 = 15,479	Lab wins
Final result	**7 seats**	**4 seats**	**3 seats**	**2 seats**	

seats in Scotland Mid and Fife, then a fairly fine-grade matching of votes to seats is possible.

Using the method set out above we computed who would have won how many local and top-up seats in each of Scotland's eight Euro-constituencies on the basis of the 1997 general election votes, and Table 3 shows the results. Overall Labour would gain the lion's share (56 out of 73 local seats), and because it was somewhat under-represented in a few areas it would also go on to gain six additional members. The Liberal Democrats would also do well locally, winning 11 seats, but gaining only five additional members, because their vote totals outside their core constituencies were not impressive. The SNP would win only six local seats (as they did for Westminster), but garner two fifths of all the additional member seats, for the first time breaking out of their historically small representation at a parliamentary level. And the Conservatives would be chasing close behind them in amassing regional seats, 22 in all to counteract their not winning in any local area.

The great advantage of using the general election to model seats is that it provides up to date information on how local alignments are patterned. But it is in fact highly unlikely that people will vote for the Scottish Parliament on exactly the same lines as they do for Westminster elections. Table 3 assumes that no one will want to split the two votes they are given in AMS,

Table 3: Seats in the Scottish Parliament won by the parties on the basis of the 1997 general election votes

Euro-Constituency		Lab	SNP	Con	Lib Dem	Other	Total
South Scotland:	Local seats	6	1	0	2	0	9
	Additional members	1	2	4	0	0	7
Highlands and Islands:	Local seats	2	1	0	5	0	8
	Additional members	2	3	2	0	0	7
Scotland Mid & Fife:	Local seats	6	2	0	1	0	9
	Additional members	1	2	3	1	0	7
Scotland North East:	Local seats	5	2	0	2	0	9
	Additional members	0	2	4	1	0	7
Glasgow:	Local seats	10	0	0	0	0	10
	Additional members	1	4	1	1	0	7
Lothians:	Local seats	8	0	0	1	0	9
	Additional members	0	3	3	1	0	7
Central Scotland:	Local seats	10	0	0	0	0	10
	Additional members	1	4	2	0	0	7
West of Scotland:	Local seats	9	0	0	0	0	9
	Additional members	0	3	3	1	0	7
PARLIAMENT	Local seats	56	6	0	11	0	73
	Additional members	6	23	22	5	0	56
	Total seats	62	29	22	16	0	129

supporting different parties in their local constituency and at the wider regional level. It also assumes that the different issues controlled by the Scottish Parliament, heavily skewed towards welfare state issues and regional economic development, make no difference to how people vote – although there is already ample evidence from local government elections that a different issue mix produces different voter alignments.

To get a better view of how people might behave, we adopt a *simulation* approach, combining evidence from a major opinion poll carried out immediately after the May 1997 general election with the evidence on constituency voting patterns afforded by the general election. ICM Research interviewed 1152 people spread fairly evenly across three regions of Scotland - the highlands; the central lowlands; and the southern uplands. Respondents were given the ballot paper shown in Figure 1 and asked:

> 'As you may know, the Labour party and the Liberal Democrats propose to establish a Scottish Parliament located in Edinburgh, which would have control over various issues such as the health service in Scotland, education, transport, housing, policing and economic development.

Suppose now you were voting for a Scottish parliament using this ballot paper. First vote for a candidate and a party that you would like to represent your local constituency.
And then, vote for a party to shape the overall balance of party seats in the Scottish Parliament. You may choose to support the same party or a different party.'

In fact Table 4 shows that there were quite high 'defection' rates across voters in all parties, perhaps reflecting tactical voting in the general election. Support for the Conservatives in the Edinburgh Parliament ballot was well down, and there were almost no transfers to them from

Table 4: How respondents backed parties on the Scottish Parliament ballot, by their vote in the 1997 general election

	Party voted for in 1997 general election:			
Vote for local seats (%)	Lab	SNP	Con	Lib Dem
Labour	79	13	4	16
Scottish National Party	11	79	8	6
Conservative	0	0	69	1
Liberal Democrats	2	6	6	74
Not sure/Don't know	8	2	12	2
Total	100%	100%	99%	99%
Vote for additional MPs (%)				
Labour	72	13	5	22
Scottish National Party	16	77	10	11
Conservative	0	1	64	1
Liberal Democrats	5	8	9	63
Not sure/Don't know	7	2	12	3
Total	100%	101%	99%	99%

voters of other parties. The most loyal voters at constituency level were those who backed Labour or SNP in the general election, but slightly more Labour voters defected in their second AMS vote for top-up MPs. Conservative supporters at the General Election were most prone to choose another party in the AMS local level ballots, but both Tory and Liberal Democrat supporters were conspicuously likely to defect in choosing additional members - with fewer than two thirds backing the party they supported in the general election.

We next took these responses and asked how local constituency results would have altered and how the support for parties at the Euro-constituency level would be patterned if all voters in each of our three regions (the Highlands, central Scotland and southern Scotland) behaved exactly as did our survey respondents. This step is obviously a simplification, but it is the best available guide to the differences that might occur in a real Scottish Parliament election under the full additional member system. We tested two ways of working out local constituency results - one involving the simple application of the regional swing to the 1997 election results in each area, and the other involving a more complex 'proportionate swing' weighting. These two methods produced slightly different results, but after examining the results we have gone ahead with the simple swing measure - whose outcomes seems more intuitively probable. To compute the party vote for each constituency we took the regional data on how our respondents would vote for additional members, applied the proportional swing calculation to each Westminster constituency and then grouped together these results into Euro constituencies. Table 5 shows how the results mapped out in seat allocations across Scotland.

At the local seats level the patterns of support in our survey would not make all that much difference. The Conservatives would just win three local constituency seats (instead of none), taking Edinburgh Pentlands, Aberdeen South and Eastwood from Labour. And the SNP would take Inverness East, Nairn and Lochaber instead of Labour. In most cases these local switches are more than offset or swamped by the changes in the party votes at Euro-constituency level, with the Tories faring much worse, cutting their additional members won across Scotland from 21 on the basis of the 1997 general election to just 13 on the basis of our survey results. Labour would stay the same in additional members, but the SNP would grow to 30 (instead of 23 on the general election basis) and the Liberal Democrats to 10 (instead of 5 on the general election basis).

Table 5: Seats in the Scottish Parliament won by the parties on the basis of the responses to the Scottish Parliament ballot form

Euro-Constituency		Lab	SNP	Con	Lib Dem	Other	Total
South Scotland:	Local seats	6	1	0	2	0	9
	Additional members	1	3	3	0	0	7
Highlands and Islands:	Local seats	1	2	0	5	0	8
	Additional members	3	3	1	0	0	7
Scotland Mid & Fife:	Local seats	6	2	0	1	0	9
	Additional members	1	3	2	1	0	7
Scotland North East:	Local seats	4	2	1	2	0	9
	Additional members	1	3	2	1	0	7
Glasgow:	Local seats	10	0	0	0	0	10
	Additional members	0	5	0	2	0	7
Lothians:	Local seats	7	0	1	1	0	9
	Additional members	0	4	3	0	0	7
Central Scotland:	Local seats	10	0	0	0	0	10
	Additional members	0	5	1	1	0	7
West of Scotland:	Local seats	8	0	1	0	0	9
	Additional members	0	4	1	2	0	7
PARLIAMENT	**Local seats**	52	7	3	11	0	73
	Additional members	6	30	10	10	0	56
	Total seats	58	37	13	21	0	129

Table 5 would produce a much more diverse multi-party Scottish parliament, with Labour four seats down, the Tories nine seats down, the Liberal Democrats five seats up, and the SNP eight seats up on the previous estimate based on general election data alone. How likely is it that the first elections to the Edinburgh Parliament will fit the pattern suggested by Table 5? A number of imponderables are involved here - such as turnout and the political dynamics in the election year itself, which may come in the mid-term of the current Labour government. But the lowered levels of support from voters backing the Conservatives on Scottish issues than in Westminster elections looks highly likely to continue - especially if the referendum convincingly endorses the parliament against lone Tory opposition. Equally the enhanced level of support our survey found for the SNP when people were choosing a Scottish assembly looks perfectly credible, especially as the SNP will clearly be the main 'opposition' party in advance of the election. A key factor in this SNP boost was the opportunity for ticket-splitting which the AMS ballot provides.

Conclusions

There are many signs in our findings that Scotland's already well-established political distinctiveness will continue to develop as the first Scottish Parliament is elected and begins its proceedings. The key party under pressure as a result will be Labour in the first instance, campaigning at a UK level against an opposition principally from the right lead by the Conservatives, but campaigning within Scotland almost inevitably in a coalition Executive with the Liberal Democrats and with a distinctive opposition of the left provided by the SNP. The Scottish and UK party systems may increasingly diverge over time, especially if Scottish voters as a whole begin to demonstrate the degree of political sophistication shown by our sample - adjusting their votes in a distinctive way when moving from Westminster elections to voting for the Edinburgh parliament, and using 'ticket-splitting' to create a more balanced and pluralistic politics in Scotland than has existed at Westminister since the 1920s. The SNP will come of age with devolution - no longer a party whose representatives can all fit in one taxi cab, but a serious political force in the Edinburgh Parliament. On current form, devolution will provide something of a way back from the wilderness for the Scottish Tories. But if our survey findings are correct, they will achieve only 'minor party' status in the Scottish Parliament, and have a great deal of work to do if they are ever to recover the status of official opposition to Labour.

3. Electing the Welsh Assembly

The new Welsh Assembly is constructed on altogether more modest lines than the Scottish Parliament. It has fewer than half the Edinburgh body's membership, with just 60 seats. Two thirds of the seats (40) comprise the existing Westminster constituencies in Wales, where the local members will be elected by the first-past-the-post method. The remaining third (20 seats) will be elected as additional members, with four members for each of Wales' five Euro-constituencies. The White Paper contains a hint that in future different arrangements might come into place for grouping constituencies. From 1999 the existing Euro-constituencies will cease to exist because the government has agreed with the Liberal Democrats to introduce a List PR system of representation - and all of Wales will then comprise a single region with five seats.

The appearance of the ballot papers will follow exactly the same lines as that for Scotland (shown in Figure 1 above), except of course that the ballot paper in our survey included Plaid Cymru instead of the SNP. To see how the new system will operate we follow essentially the same procedures as set out above for Scotland, but modified of course to take account of the distinctive features of the Welsh system. Table 6 shows the much shorter process involved in allocating the four additional members in Wales, using as an example the Wales North Euro-constituency, and the votes cast there in the 1997 General Election for the main parties. Labour was well ahead of the other parties in terms of votes, but would win 7 out of the 9 local seats in this area. The Conservatives ran second but won no local seats, while the Liberal Democrats also won no local seats despite running a close fourth to Plaid Cymru, who won two local seats. The allocation of additional members begins by awarding the Tories the first top-up seat, and then the second one as well. The Liberal Democrats take the third seat to give them some representation, but then the Tories narrowly win the fourth and last additional member. There the Welsh system stops - leaving Labour with one seat for every 23,500 votes; Plaid Cymru, with one seat for every 24,950 votes; the Tories with one seat for every 28,500 votes - but the Liberal Democrats with only one seat to show for their 41,500 votes. Unlike the Scottish system, with its greater number of additional members, the Welsh system can easily leave very marked disparities in representation amongst the parties uncorrected. In most cases we shall see that this effect works to benefit the

Labour and Conservative parties, and reduces the representation of the Liberal Democrats and of Plaid Cymru (especially in south Wales).

Table 6: How the AMS system would work in Wales, using the 1997 results for the Wales North Constituency

	Labour	Conservative	Paid Cymru	Liberal Dem	Additional member result
Party vote	164,664	85,554	49,904	41,517	
Local seats	7	0	2	0	
1st division	/8 = 20,583	/1 = 85,554	/3 = 16,634	/1 = 41,517	Con wins
2nd division	/8 = 20,583	/2 = 42,777	/3 = 16,634	/1 = 41,517	Con wins
3rd division	/8 = 20,583	/3 = 28,518	/3 = 16,634	/1 = 41,517	Lib wins
4th division	/8 = 20,583	/3 = 28,518	/3 = 16,634	/2 = 20,758	Con wins
Final result	7 seats	3 seats	2 seats	1 seats	

To appreciate how the system would map out across Wales as a whole we can use the 1997 general election results across Westminster constituencies to give the local results, and aggregate those votes up to the level of the five Euro constituencies to give the party votes on which the additional member allocations take place. Again it is important to emphasize that this is an artificial exercise, which assumes that everyone would vote just as they did in May 1997; that turnout levels would be the same; and that everyone would cast identical votes for local seat candidates and for parties at the Euro-constituency level. We shall see below that varying the last assumption makes a difference to outcomes. With these cautions in mind, Table 7 shows the results.

Labour emerges with a clear majority in the Assembly on local seats alone on this basis, winning 85 per cent of them. But because of the fragmentation of the non-Labour votes between three other parties, and of the "big party" bias of the d'Hondt allocation system, Labour also picks up three additional member seats (in Wales Mid and West, and in both South-East and South West Wales, despite holding all the local seats in these two areas). The Conservatives would win no local seats on this basis, just as they won no Westminster constituencies in 1997. But the Tories would win two thirds of all the additional member seats to make them easily the second party in the Assembly and would clearly become the official opposition, if the Assembly runs on

Table 7: Seats in the Welsh Assembly won by the parties on the basis of the 1997 general election votes

Euro-Constituency		Lab	Con	Lib Dem	Plaid Cymru	Other	Total
Wales North.	Local seats	7	0	0	2	0	9
	Additional members	0	3	1	0	0	4
Wales Mid & West:	Local seats	4	0	2	2	0	8
	Additional members	1	3	0	0	0	4
South Wales West:	Local seats	7	0	0	0	0	7
	Additional members	1	2	1	0	0	4
South Wales East:	Local seats	8	0	0	0	0	8
	Additional members	1	2	1	0	0	4
South Wales Central:	Local seats	8	0	0	0	0	8
	Additional members	0	3	1	0	0	4
ASSEMBLY	**Local seats**	34	0	2	4	0	40
	Additional members	3	13	4	0	0	20
	Total seats	37	13	6	4	0	60

Westminster lines. Thus politics in Cardiff might well come to seem a mini-image of Westminster, with a majority Labour executive facing a small Conservative opposition, but one still enjoying 'major party' status. The Liberal Democrats would win two local seats, and four more additional members, but have less than half the Tory numbers. And Plaid Cymru would have no more Cardiff representatives than it has Westminster MPs - in particular missing out completely on any additional member representation, perhaps a problematic outcome in legitimacy terms if it were to occur in real life.

However, as in Scotland, there are good grounds for believing that voters will not be aligned in relation to the Assembly on exactly the same lines as they are for Westminster elections. The Conservatives in Wales are unlikely to incur the same opprobrium for opposing devolution as they have done in Scotland, and so their Assembly representation may not change as dramatically as it did there. But differences are still likely - for example, because voters want to curb the size or predominance of the Labour bloc in the Assembly, or are prepared to vote Plaid Cymru or Liberal Democrat in the Assembly elections, perhaps to ensure that south Wales interests alone do not settle all policy issues. To see whether such speculations have any weight, we look at the responses of 622 people interviewed by ICM Research immediately after the general election, chosen to be a representative sample of opinion in two regions, middle and northern Wales, and southern Wales. We asked them to vote again for the Assembly, using the same form of words as we cite above for Scotland, (but obviously with 'Welsh Assembly' and 'Cardiff' included instead of the Scottish references). Table 8 shows how Wales respondents would choose their Assembly members, by their vote in the 1997 general election.

As in Scotland people who voted for the Liberal Democrats in 1997 were the most likely to defect to one of the other parties in the Assembly elections. At the constituency level Plaid Cymru voters were the most loyal, but they showed a small tendency to defect to Labour in the

Table 8: How respondents backed parties on the Welsh Assembly ballot, by their vote in the 1997 general election

Party voted for in 1997 general election:

Vote for local seats (%)	Lab	Con	Lib Dem	Plaid Cymru
Labour	79	2	9	4
Conservative	1	74	3	2
Liberal Democrats	3	10	66	2
Plaid Cymru	11	7	19	83
Not sure/Don't know	6	8	3	10
Total	100%	101%	100%	101%
Vote for additional MPs (%)				
Labour	76	1	7	14
Conservative	1	71	3	4
Liberal Democrats	7	10	66	4
Plaid Cymru	9	9	20	71
Not sure/Don't know	6	8	3	8
Total	99%	99%	99%	101%

party vote stage of the AMS ballot. Labour voters were very loyal on both stages of the ballot, but their biggest defections were to Plaid Cymru. And since Labour voters were more than half of the total (274 out of 492 respondents giving complete answers), this change has real significance in boosting Plaid Cymru's support at constituency level and in party votes. Tory voters were much more loyal in completing the Assembly ballot than their counterparts in Scotland, but one tenth of them switched to the Liberal Democrats and slightly fewer to Plaid Cymru.

To trace out the implications of these smaller shifts in support for parties in the Assembly elections, Table 9 shows the revised local and top-up seats results across all the five Welsh Euro-constituencies using our survey responses to remodel local constituency results and the party votes used for allocating additional members. (As in Scotland we again compared a simple swing and more complex proportional swing measure for local seats, producing very similar outcomes but with some small differences. The party vote is calculated on a proportional swing basis for the Westminster constituencies and then aggregated up to the Euro-constituency level)

As in Scotland, there would be only small changes on the basis of our survey findings in which parties won local constituencies. Labour would lose three local seats if our simulations were correct: Conwy to the Liberal Democrats, Clwyd West to the Conservatives, and Camarthen to Plaid Cymru - but in all these cases a very narrow margin of votes would be involved, well within the margin of error of our survey. The really interesting changes take place in the additional member seats, with Plaid Cymru winning three seats to add to its five local seats, and thus getting twice as many Assembly members as in the earlier scenario. The Conservatives would pick up four fewer Assembly seats at the additional member stage, and the Liberal Democrats would stay the same (but with one extra local seat).

In overall terms if our survey responses provide a better guide to the Assembly's composition than relying on the 1997 general election results alone, then there would be changes, but not as great as in Scotland. Labour's majority would be somewhat reduced, and Plaid Cymru would be much more prominent, very closely rivaling the Tories, and with the Liberal Democrats just behind them. The Assembly would be structured much more on the lines of Welsh Labour versus a multi-party opposition than on classic two-party system lines.

Table 9: Seats in the Welsh Assembly won by the parties on the basis of responses to the Welsh Assembly ballot form

Euro-Constituency		Lab	Con	Lib Dem	Plaid Cymru	Other	Total
Wales North:	Local seats	5	1	1	2	0	9
	Additional members	2	2	0	0	0	4
Wales Mid & West:	Local seats	3	0	2	3	0	8
	Additional members	2	2	0	0	0	4
South Wales West:	Local seats	7	0	0	0	0	7
	Additional members	0	1	2	1	0	4
South Wales East:	Local seats	8	0	0	0	0	8
	Additional members	0	2	1	1	0	4
South Wales Central:	Local seats	8	0	0	0	0	8
	Additional members	0	2	1	1	0	4
ASSEMBLY	Local seats	31	1	3	5	0	40
	Additional members	4	9	4	3	0	20
	Total seats	35	10	7	8	0	60

Conclusions

Voting patterns in Wales have not developed the degree of separateness which already distinguish Scottish politics. But there are good grounds for believing that the Assembly elections will produce significant variations from Westminster voting patterns, which will reduce the Conservatives' prominence and increase that of Plaid Cymru. Given Labour's strength in the 1997 general election, and its buoyant opinion poll leads in government so far (until autumn 1997), an outright Labour majority still seems likely in the Welsh Assembly. One key support of Labour dominance is the rather limited degree of proportionality which will be achieved under the Welsh Assembly schema, given the choice of a d'Hondt voting rule to allocate the top-up seats. One option which election reformers of all parties might like to advocate during the legislative phase of creating a Welsh Assembly is a modest increase in the total number of representatives to 65. This change would allow a fifth additional member to be allocated in each Euro-constituency and would significantly increase the proportionality of the overall election outcomes.

About the Democratic Audit

The Democratic Audit of the United Kingdom is the title of a project that in inquiring into the quality of democracy and political freedoms in the UK. The Audit monitors democracy and political freedom in Britain through a series of reports at regular intervals.

The Audit publishes up to six reports on democratic and human rights issues every year. The most well-known are the path-breaking studies of quangos in the United Kingdom, one of which was published in conjunction with a *Dispatches* documentary on Channel 4 TV. You can an annual subscriber for £35 p.a. (institutions, £50). Or you can order reports individually from the Scarman Trust, Exmouth House, 3-11 Pine Street, London EC1R 0JH. Prices include packing and postage. All Democratic Audit papers are published jointly by the Scarman Trust and the Human Rights Centre, University of Essex.

In September 1996, the Audit published its first major report, *The Three Pillars of Liberty* (by Francesca Klug, Keir Starmer and Stuart Weir; Routledge), on the protection of political and civil rights in the United Kingdom. The proceedings of the conference on issues arising from *The Three Pillars* (with contributions from Helena Kennedy QC, Professor Richard Falk, Alun Michael MP and Professor Philip Alston, chairperson of the UN Committee on Economic, Social and Cultural Rights) are published in a special human rights issue of *Political Quarterly* (vol 68, No. 2, April-June 1997).

The Audit has also recently published *Modernising Britain's Democracy: why, what and how*, by Andrew Adonis, the *Observer* columnist. This pamphlet argues the case for democratic change in the United Kingdom.

The second major Democratic Audit report is on accountability and openness in British government and will be published next summer by Routledge. The Audit is also preparing an International Almanac on Elections and Voting for the forthcoming referendum on electoral systems in the United Kingdom, and a benchmark report on economic and social rights in the UK. Democratic Audit packs - teaching aids for education in democracy and freedom - are being developed for use both in international seminars for practitioners and secondary schools in the UK.

The intention is to follow up these two authoritative "landmark" studies with further studies at intervals of three to five years, so that the quality of democracy and political freedoms in the UK can be measured over time. The purpose is to enable the public to judge whether this country is becoming more or less democratic and free. The current plan is to publish the first follow-up reports on Britain at the end of this Labour government's term in office.

The Audit is sponsored by the Joseph Rowntree Charitable Trust and is based at the Human Rights Centre, University of Essex. But scholars and specialists from other universities and institutions are co-operating as "auditors" and advisers on the project. The Audit undertakes consultancy and educational work in the UK and abroad, and organises international seminars on democracy and freedom. It is currently developing a project to "universalise" the criteria used for its auditing purposes.

The director of the Audit is Stuart Weir, a Senior Research Fellow at Essex. Professor Kevin Boyle, director of the Human Rights Centre at Essex, is overall academic editor of Audit publications and Professor David Beetham, Department of Politics, Leeds University, acts as consultant. The Audit has a small steering committee, under the chairmanship of Professor Boyle and David Shutt, chairperson of the Charitable Trust's democratic panel.

Please send any comments you may have on this or any other Democratic Audit publication to:-

Professor Kevin Boyle,
Human Rights Centre,
University of Essex,
Wivenhoe Park,
Colchester, Essex
CO4 3SQ